everyday
Family
favourites

everyday Family favourites

MURDOCH
BOOKS

contents

soups

ROAST PUMPKIN SOUP

Preparation time: 20 minutes
Total cooking time: 55 minutes
Serves 6

1.25 kg (2 lb 8 oz) pumpkin, peeled
    and cut into chunks
2 tablespoons olive oil
1 large onion, chopped
2 teaspoons ground cumin
1 large carrot, chopped
1 celery stick, chopped
1 litre chicken or vegetable stock
sour cream, to serve
finely chopped fresh parsley, to serve
ground nutmeg, to serve

1 Preheat the oven to moderate 180°C (350°F/Gas 4). Place the pumpkin chunks on a greased baking tray and lightly brush with half the olive oil. Bake for 25 minutes, or until the pumpkin is softened and slightly browned around the edges.

2 Heat the remaining oil in a large saucepan. Cook the onion and cumin for 2 minutes, then add the carrot and celery and cook for 3 minutes more, stirring frequently. Add the roasted pumpkin and stock. Bring to the boil, then reduce the heat and simmer for 20 minutes.

3 Allow to cool a little then purée in batches in a blender or food processor. Return the soup to the pan and gently reheat without boiling. Season to taste with salt and cracked black pepper. Top with sour cream and sprinkle with chopped parsley and ground nutmeg before serving.

NUTRITION PER SERVE
Protein 5 g; Fat 8.5 g, Carbohydrate 15 g; Dietary Fibre 3.5 g; Cholesterol 4.5 mg; 665 kJ (160 Cal)

NOTE: Butternut pumpkin is often used in soups as it has a sweeter flavour than other varieties.

HINT: If the soup is too thick, thin it down with a little stock.

Lightly brush the pumpkin chunks with oil and bake until softened.

Transfer the cooled mixture to a blender or food processor and purée in batches.

PEA AND HAM SOUP

Preparation time: 15 minutes +
   overnight soaking
Total cooking time: 2 hours,
   10 minutes
Serves 8

500 g (1 lb) yellow or green split peas
1 leek
1 tablespoon oil
2 carrots, chopped
1 celery stick, chopped
2 cloves garlic, crushed
750 g (1½ lb) meaty ham bone

1 Put the split peas in a large bowl, cover with water and soak overnight.
2 Cut the leek in half lengthways and wash thoroughly in cold water to remove any dirt. Slice thickly. Heat the oil in a large heavy-based pan, and add the leek, carrot, celery and garlic. Cook, stirring, for 2–3 minutes, then add the drained peas, the ham bone and 2.5 litres water. Bring to the boil, then reduce the heat and simmer for 2 hours, stirring occasionally.
3 Remove the ham bone and set it aside to cool. Cool the soup a little then purée in batches in a blender or food processor and return to the

pan. Remove the meat from the bone, chop and return the meat to the soup. Season to taste with salt and black pepper, reheat gently and serve hot.

NUTRITION PER SERVE
Protein 17 g; Fat 8 g; Carbohydrate 8.5 g;
Dietary Fibre 4 g; Cholesterol 30 mg;
725 kJ (175 Cal)

NOTE: If you forget to soak the split peas overnight, rinse them and cook the soup until the peas are tender.

Soak the split peas in water overnight, then drain before adding to the soup.

Add the peas, ham bone and water to the pan and bring to the boil.

Remove the meat from the bone and cut into small chunks.

FRENCH ONION SOUP

Preparation time: 30 minutes
Total cooking time: 1 hour 30 minutes
Serves 4

50 g (1¾ oz) butter
1 tablespoon olive oil
1 kg (2 lb) onions, thinly sliced into
    rings
3 x 420 g (14 oz) cans chicken or beef
    consommé
½ cup (125 ml/4 fl oz) dry sherry
½ French bread stick
⅓ cup (35 g/1¼ oz) grated Parmesan
1 cup (125 g/4 oz) finely grated
    Cheddar or Gruyère
1 tablespoon finely chopped fresh
    parsley, to serve

1 Heat the butter and oil in a large
saucepan, then add the onion and
cook, stirring frequently, over low heat
for 45 minutes, or until softened and
translucent. Do not rush this stage—
cook the onion thoroughly so that it
caramelises and the flavours develop.
2 Add the consommé, sherry and
1 cup (250 ml/8 fl oz) water. Bring
to the boil, then reduce the heat and
simmer for 30 minutes. Season to taste.
3 Meanwhile, slice the bread into four
thick slices and arrange them in a single
layer under a hot grill. Toast one side,
turn and sprinkle with Parmesan, and
toast until crisp and golden and the
cheese has melted.
4 Put the bread slices into serving
bowls. Ladle in the hot soup, sprinkle
with the cheese and parsley and serve.

NUTRITION PER SERVE
Protein 20 g; Fat 30 g; Carbohydrate 30 g;
Dietary Fibre 5 g; Cholesterol 70 mg;
1925 kJ (460 Cal)

Using a large sharp knife, cut the onions into
thin rings.

Heat the oil and butter in a large pan and add
the onion.

Stir frequently over low heat until the onion is
softened and translucent.

CHICKEN NOODLE SOUP

Preparation time: 15 minutes
  + 1 hour refrigeration
Total cooking time: 1 hour 20 minutes
Serves 4–6

1.25 kg (2¹/₂ lb) chicken wings
2 celery sticks, chopped
1 carrot, chopped
1 onion, chopped
1 bay leaf
1 fresh thyme sprig
4 fresh parsley sprigs
45 g (1¹/₂ oz) dried fine egg noodles
250 g (8 oz) chicken breast fillets,
  finely chopped
2 tablespoons chopped fresh parsley
chopped fresh chives, to serve

1 Rinse the chicken wings and place in a large pan with the celery, carrot, onion, bay leaf, thyme, parsley, 1 teaspoon salt and 2 litres of water. Bring to the boil slowly, skimming the surface as required. Simmer, covered, for 1 hour. Allow to cool slightly, then strain and discard the chicken and vegetables.
2 Cool the stock further, then cover and refrigerate for at least 1 hour, or until fat forms on the surface of the stock and can be spooned off.
3 Place the stock in a large pan and bring to the boil. Gently crush the noodles and add to the soup. Return to the boil and simmer for 8 minutes, or until tender. Add the chopped chicken and parsley and simmer for a further 4–5 minutes, or until the chicken is cooked through. Serve topped with the chives.

NUTRITION PER SERVE (6)
Protein 45 g; Fat 8 g; Carbohydrate 8 g;
Dietary Fibre 2 g; Cholesterol 135 mg;
1205 kJ (290 cal)

Using a skimmer or slotted spoon, skim the surface of the stock as required.

Using a spoon, remove the fat that forms on the surface of the chilled stock.

Add the crushed noodles, then simmer for 8 minutes, or until tender.

CREAM OF ASPARAGUS SOUP

Preparation time: 20 minutes
Total cooking time: 55 minutes
Serves 4–6

1 kg (2 lb) asparagus spears
30 g (1 oz) butter
1 onion, finely chopped
1 litre (32 fl oz) vegetable stock
1/4 cup (7 g/1/4 oz) basil leaves,
    chopped
1 teaspoon celery salt
1 cup (250 ml/8 fl oz) cream

1 Break off the woody ends from the asparagus (hold both ends of the spear and bend it gently—the woody end will snap off and can be thrown away) and trim off the tips. Blanch the tips in boiling water for 1–2 minutes, refresh in cold water and set aside. Chop the asparagus stems into large pieces.
2 Melt the butter in a large pan and cook the onion for 3–4 minutes over medium-low heat, or until soft and golden. Add the chopped asparagus stems and cook for 1–2 minutes, stirring continuously.
3 Add the stock, basil and celery salt. Bring to the boil, reduce the heat and simmer, covered, for 30 minutes.
4 Check that the asparagus is well cooked and soft. If not, simmer for a further 10 minutes. Set aside and allow to cool slightly.
5 Pour into a processor and process in batches until smooth. Then sieve into a clean pan. Return to the heat, pour in the cream and gently reheat. Do not allow the soup to boil. Season to taste with salt and white pepper. Add the asparagus tips and serve immediately.

NUTRITION PER SERVE (6)
Protein 6 g; Fat 22 g; Carbohydrate 5 g;
Dietary Fibre 3 g; Cholesterol 70 mg;
990 kJ (237 cal)

HINT: If you are not using home-made stock, always taste before adding seasoning to your soup—shop-bought stock can be very salty.

The woody end from the asparagus spear will snap off when you bend the spear.

Test whether the asparagus is well cooked by piercing it with a fork.

OXTAIL SOUP

Preparation time: 20 minutes + chilling
Total cooking time: 3 hours 20 minutes
Serves 4

1 tablespoon plain flour
1 kg (2 lb) oxtail, chopped into 5 cm
    (2 inch) pieces (ask your butcher
    to do this)
1 tablespoon oil
2 litres beef stock
1 onion, chopped
1 celery stick, chopped
2 carrots, chopped
1 swede or turnip, peeled and
    chopped
3 whole cloves
12 peppercorns

2 bay leaves
1 tablespoon plain flour, extra
2 tablespoons port
1 tablespoon tomato paste
1/3 cup (20 g/3/4 oz) finely chopped
    fresh parsley

1 Season the flour, put it in a plastic bag with the oxtail and shake to coat. Shake off excess flour. Heat the oil in a large pan, add the oxtail and cook in batches, tossing continually, for 5 minutes, or until evenly browned. Return all the oxtail to the pan.
2 Add the stock, 1 1/2 cups (375 ml/ 12 fl oz) water, vegetables, cloves, peppercorns, bay leaves and 1/2 teaspoon salt. Bring slowly to the boil then reduce the heat and simmer, covered, for 3 hours.

3 Strain the vegetables and meat, reserving the liquid. Discard the vegetables and leave the meat to cool. Pull the meat from the bone, shred and refrigerate. Meanwhile, refrigerate the stock until the fat has solidified on the surface and can be removed with a spoon. Add the meat.
4 Put the soup in a clean pan. Mix together the extra flour, port and tomato paste, and add to the pan. Bring to the boil, stirring, until the soup thickens slightly. Simmer for 10 minutes, then stir in the parsley.

NUTRITION PER SERVE
Protein 25 g; Fat 7.5 g; Carbohydrate 9.5 g;
Dietary Fibre 2.5 g; Cholesterol 65 mg;
1700 kJ (405 Cal)

Put the seasoned flour and oxtail pieces in a plastic bag and shake to coat.

Heat the oil and cook the oxtail pieces in batches until browned.

Use a spoon to remove the solidified fat from the surface of the stock.

CHICKEN AND CORN SOUP

Preparation time: 15 minutes
Total cooking time: 20 minutes
Serves 6

3 corn cobs
1 tablespoon oil
4 spring onions, finely chopped
2 teaspoons grated fresh ginger
1 litre chicken stock
1 tablespoon rice wine, mirin or sherry
1 tablespoon soy sauce
1/2 small barbecued chicken, shredded

1 tablespoon cornflour
1 teaspoon sesame oil
420 g (13 oz) can creamed corn
fresh thyme sprigs, to garnish

1 Cut the corn kernels from the cobs—you will need about 2 cups (400 g/13 oz). Heat the oil in a large pan, and add the spring onion and ginger. Cook for 1 minute, or until softened, then add the corn, stock, rice wine and soy sauce. Bring slowly to the boil, then reduce the heat and simmer for 10 minutes, or until the corn is cooked through. Add the chicken.
2 In a bowl, blend the cornflour with 3 tablespoons water or stock to make

a smooth paste. Add to the soup with the sesame oil and simmer, stirring constantly, until slightly thickened. Stir in the creamed corn and heat for 2–3 minutes without allowing to boil. Season and serve hot, garnished with the thyme sprigs.

NUTRITION PER SERVE
Protein 14 g; Fat 8 g; Carbohydrate 30 g;
Dietary Fibre 5 g; Cholesterol 45 mg;
1077 kJ (255 Cal)

NOTE: If fresh corn is unavailable, use a 440 g (14 oz) can of drained corn kernels.

Use a fork to shred the meat from the barbecued chicken.

Remove the husks from the corn cobs and cut off the kernels.

Blend the cornflour and water or stock to make a smooth paste.

pasta & noodles

LASAGNE

Preparation time: 40 minutes
Total cooking time: 1 hour 35 minutes
Serves 8

2 teaspoons olive oil
1 large onion, chopped
2 carrots, finely chopped
2 celery sticks, finely chopped
2 zucchini, finely chopped
2 cloves garlic, crushed
500 g (1 lb) lean beef mince
2 x 400 g (13 oz) cans crushed
    tomatoes
1/2 cup (125 ml/4 fl oz) beef stock
2 tablespoons tomato paste
2 teaspoons dried oregano
375 g (12 oz) instant or fresh lasagne
    sheets

CHEESE SAUCE
3 cups (750 ml/24 fl oz) skim milk
1/3 cup (40 g/1 1/4 oz) cornflour
100 g (3 1/2 oz) reduced-fat cheese,
    grated

1 Heat the olive oil in a large non-stick frying pan. Add the onion and cook for 5 minutes, or until soft. Add the carrot, celery and zucchini and cook, stirring constantly, for 5 minutes, or until the vegetables are soft. Add the garlic and cook for another minute. Add the mince and cook over high heat, stirring, until browned. Break up any lumps with a wooden spoon.
2 Add the crushed tomato, beef stock, tomato paste and dried oregano to the pan and stir to thoroughly combine. Bring the mixture to the boil, then reduce the heat and simmer gently, partially covered, for 20 minutes, stirring occasionally to prevent the mixture sticking to the pan.

3 Preheat the oven to moderate 180°C (350°F/Gas 4). Spread a little of the meat sauce into the base of a 23 cm x 30 cm (9 inch x 12 inch) ovenproof dish. Arrange a layer of lasagne sheets in the dish, breaking some of the sheets, if necessary, to fit in neatly.
4 Spread half the meat sauce over the top to cover evenly. Cover with another layer of lasagne sheets, a layer of meat sauce, then a final layer of lasagne sheets.
5 To make the cheese sauce, blend a little of the milk with the cornflour, to form a smooth paste, in a small pan. Gradually blend in the remaining milk and stir constantly over low heat until the mixture boils and thickens. Remove from the heat and stir in the grated cheese until melted. Spread evenly over the top of the lasagne and bake for 1 hour.
6 Check the lasagne after 25 minutes. If the top is browning too quickly, cover loosely with non-stick baking paper or foil. Take care when removing the baking paper or foil that the topping does not come away with the paper. Leave the lasagne to stand for 15 minutes before cutting into portions for serving.

NUTRITION PER SERVE
Protein 15 g; Fat 12 g; Carbohydrate 50 g;
Dietary Fibre 5 g; Cholesterol 10 mg;
1885 kJ (450 Cal)

STORAGE TIME: Can be frozen for up to 2–3 months. When required, thaw overnight in the refrigerator, then reheat, covered with foil, for about 30 minutes in a moderate oven.

Chop the garlic and crush using the flat side of a large knife.

Add the vegetables to the pan and stir constantly until soft.

When you add the meat, break up any lumps with a wooden spoon.

Spread a little of the meat sauce over the base and cover evenly with lasagne sheets.

Remove the pan from the heat and stir in the cheese until melted.

Spread the cheese sauce evenly over the top of the lasagne.

PASTA CARBONARA

Preparation time: 15 minutes
Total cooking time: 25 minutes
Serves 4–6

8 bacon rashers
500 g (1 lb) pasta
4 eggs
1¼ cups (315 ml/10 fl oz) cream
½ cup (60 g/2 oz) grated Parmesan

1 Remove the bacon rind and cut the bacon into thin strips. Cook over medium heat until crisp. Drain on paper towels. Meanwhile, cook the pasta in a large pan of rapidly boiling salted water until *al dente*. Drain well and return to the pan.

2 Beat the eggs, cream and Parmesan together and season well. Stir in the bacon. Pour over the hot pasta in the saucepan and toss gently until the sauce coats the pasta. Return to very low heat and cook for about 1 minute, or until the sauce has thickened slightly. Don't increase the heat or the eggs will scramble. Season with black pepper and serve immediately with extra grated Parmesan.

NUTRITION PER SERVE (6)
Protein 22 g; Fat 36 g; Carbohydrate 60 g;
Dietary Fibre 4 g; Cholesterol 213.5 mg;
2700 kJ (645 cal)

Cook the bacon strips, stirring, until they are crisp, being careful not to let them burn.

After beating together the eggs, cream and Parmesan, stir in the cooked bacon.

SPAGHETTI WITH MEATBALLS

Preparation time: 40 minutes
Total cooking time: 30 minutes
Serves 4

MEATBALLS
500 g (1 lb) beef mince
1/2 cup (40 g/1 1/4 oz) fresh
    breadcrumbs
1 onion, finely chopped
2 cloves garlic, crushed
2 teaspoons Worcestershire sauce
1 teaspoon dried oregano
1/4 cup (30 g/1 oz) plain flour
2 tablespoons olive oil

SAUCE
2 x 400 g (13 oz) cans chopped
    tomatoes
1 tablespoon olive oil
1 onion, finely chopped
2 cloves garlic, crushed
2 tablespoons tomato paste
1/2 cup (125 ml/4 fl oz) beef stock
2 teaspoons sugar

500 g (1 lb) spaghetti
grated Parmesan, to serve

1 Combine the mince, breadcrumbs, onion, garlic, Worcestershire sauce and oregano and season to taste. Use your hands to mix the ingredients well. Roll level tablespoons of the mixture into balls, dust lightly with the flour and shake off the excess. Heat the oil in a deep frying pan and cook the meatballs in batches, turning often, until browned all over. Drain well.
2 To make the sauce, purée the tomatoes in a food processor or blender. Heat the oil in the cleaned frying pan. Add the onion and cook over medium heat for a few minutes until soft and lightly golden. Add the garlic and cook for 1 minute more. Add the puréed tomatoes, tomato paste, stock and sugar to the pan and

stir to combine. Bring the mixture to the boil, and add the meatballs. Reduce the heat and simmer for 15 minutes, turning the meatballs once. Season with salt and pepper.
3 Meanwhile, cook the spaghetti in a large pan of boiling water until just tender. Drain, divide among serving plates and top with the meatballs and sauce. Serve with grated Parmesan.

NUTRITION PER SERVE
Protein 45 g; Fat 30 g; Carbohydrate 112 g;
Dietary Fibre 11 g; Cholesterol 85 mg;
3875 kJ (925 Cal)

With clean hands, roll the mixture into balls and dust with flour.

Cook the meatballs in batches, turning frequently, until browned all over.

FRIED RICE NOODLES

Preparation time: 30 minutes
Total cooking time: 15 minutes
Serves 4

2 Chinese dried pork sausages (see NOTE)
2 tablespoons oil
2 cloves garlic, finely chopped
1 onion, finely chopped
3 red chillies, seeded and chopped
250 g (8 oz) Chinese barbecued pork, finely chopped
200 g (6½ oz) peeled raw prawns
500 g (1 lb) fresh thick rice noodles, gently separated
150 g (5 oz) garlic chives, cut into 3 cm (1¼ inch) pieces

2 tablespoons kecap manis
3 eggs, lightly beaten
1 tablespoon rice vinegar
100 g (3½ oz) bean sprouts, straggly ends removed

1 Diagonally slice the dried pork sausages into paper-thin slices. Heat the oil in a large wok. Fry the sausage, tossing regularly, until golden and very crisp. Using a slotted spoon, remove from the wok and leave to drain on paper towels.
2 Reheat the oil in the wok, add the garlic, onion, chilli and pork and stir-fry for 2 minutes. Add the prawns and toss constantly, until the prawns change colour.
3 Add the noodles, chives and kecap manis and toss. Cook for 1 minute or until the noodles begin to soften. Pour the combined eggs and vinegar over the top of the noodles and toss for 1 minute. Be careful not to overcook the noodles, or let the egg-coated noodles burn on the base of the wok. Toss in the bean sprouts.
4 Arrange on a large serving platter, scatter the sausage over the top and toss a little to mix a few slices among the noodles. Serve immediately.

NUTRITION PER SERVE
Protein 47 g; Fat 17 g; Carbohydrate 30 g; Dietary Fibre 3 g; Cholesterol 285 mg; 1996 kJ (470 cal)

NOTE: Chinese pork sausages (*lup chiang*) must always be cooked before eating.

Chop the Chinese barbecued pork into very small pieces, using a sharp knife.

Remove the crisp Chinese sausage slices from the wok and drain on paper towels.

Pour the combined eggs and vinegar over the top of the noodles and toss.

MACARONI CHEESE

Preparation time: 15 minutes
Total cooking time: 35 minutes
Serves 4

225 g (7 oz) macaroni
80 g (2³/₄ oz) butter
1 onion, finely chopped
3 tablespoons plain flour
2 cups (500 ml/16 fl oz) milk
2 teaspoons wholegrain mustard
250 g (8 oz) Cheddar, grated
30 g (1 oz) fresh breadcrumbs

1 Cook the pasta in rapidly boiling salted water until *al dente*. Drain.

Preheat the oven to moderate 180°C (350°F/Gas 4) and grease a casserole.
2 Melt the butter in a large pan over low heat and cook the onion for 5 minutes, or until softened. Stir in the flour and cook for 1 minute, or until pale and foaming. Remove from the heat and gradually stir in the milk. Return to the heat and stir until the sauce boils and thickens. Reduce the heat and simmer for 2 minutes. Stir in the mustard and about three-quarters of the cheese. Season to taste.
3 Mix the pasta with the cheese sauce. Spoon into the dish and sprinkle the breadcrumbs and remaining cheese over the top. Bake for 15 minutes, or until golden brown and bubbling.

NUTRITION PER SERVE
Protein 30 g; Fat 45 g; Carbohydrate 60 g;
Dietary Fibre 4 g; Cholesterol 130 mg;
3087 kJ (737 Cal)

Cook the onion in the butter over medium heat until softened.

SALMON AND PASTA MORNAY

Preparation time: 10 minutes
Total cooking time: 15 minutes
Serves 4

400 g (13 oz) small shell pasta
30 g (1 oz) butter
6 spring onions, chopped
2 cloves garlic, crushed
1 tablespoon plain flour
1 cup (250 ml/8 fl oz) milk
1 cup (250 g/8 oz) sour cream
1 tablespoon lemon juice
425 g (14 oz) can salmon, drained and
    flaked
1/2 cup (15 g/1/2 oz) chopped fresh
    parsley

1 Cook the pasta in a large pan of rapidly boiling salted water until *al dente*. Drain and return to the pan to keep warm.
2 Meanwhile, melt the butter in a pan and cook the onion and garlic over low heat for 3 minutes or until soft. Add the flour and stir for 1 minute. Mix together the milk, cream and lemon juice and slowly add to the pan, stirring constantly. Stir over medium heat for 3 minutes or until the sauce boils and thickens.
3 Add the salmon and parsley to the sauce and stir for 1 minute to heat through. Toss with the pasta and season before serving.

NUTRITION PER SERVE
Protein 39 g; Fat 42 g; Carbohydrate 78 g;
Dietary Fibre 6 g; Cholesterol 192 mg;
3530 kJ (852 cal)

STORAGE: The sauce can be kept for up to a day, covered in the fridge. Cook the pasta and reheat the sauce just before serving.
VARIATION: Use canned tuna instead of salmon. Add 1 teaspoon of mustard to the sauce.

Combine the milk, cream and lemon juice and stir slowly into the sauce.

Once the sauce is cooked, add the drained pasta to the pan and toss well.

CHICKEN MEATBALLS

Preparation time: 15 minutes
Total cooking time: 30 minutes
Serves 6

500 g (1 lb) chicken mince
3 tablespoons fresh breadcrumbs
2 teaspoons finely chopped fresh
    thyme
1 tablespoon oil
1 onion, finely chopped
2 x 425 g (14 oz) cans diced tomatoes
2 teaspoons balsamic vinegar
1 cup (250 ml/8 fl oz) chicken stock
grated Parmesan, to serve

1 Combine the chicken mince, breadcrumbs and thyme in a large bowl and season well. Roll tablespoons of the mixture between your hands to make meatballs.
2 Heat the oil in a large non-stick frying pan and cook the meatballs in batches for 5–8 minutes, or until golden brown. Remove from the pan and drain well on paper towels.
3 Add the onion to the pan and cook for 2–3 minutes, or until softened. Add the tomato, vinegar and stock, return the meatballs to the pan, then reduce the heat and simmer for 10 minutes, or until the sauce thickens and the meatballs are cooked through. Serve with pasta and a little Parmesan.

NUTRITION PER SERVE
Protein 20 g; Fat 8.5 g; Carbohydrate 7.5 g;
Dietary Fibre 2 g; Cholesterol 42 mg;
812 kJ (194 cal)

Roll tablespoonfuls of the mixture between your hands to make meatballs.

Fry the meatballs in batches until golden brown, then drain well on paper towels.

Return the meatballs to the pan and simmer in the tomato sauce for 10 minutes.

SPINACH AND RICOTTA CANNELLONI

Preparation time: 1 hour
Total cooking time: 1 hour 15 minutes
Serves 4–6

375 g (12 oz) fresh lasagne sheets
2 tablespoons olive oil
1 large onion, finely chopped
1–2 cloves garlic, crushed
2 large bunches English spinach, finely
  chopped
650 g (1 lb 5 oz) ricotta, beaten
2 eggs, beaten
1/4 teaspoon freshly ground nutmeg
150 g (5 oz) grated mozzarella

TOMATO SAUCE
1 tablespoon olive oil
1 onion, chopped
2 cloves garlic, finely chopped
500 g (1 lb) ripe tomatoes, chopped
2 tablespoons tomato paste
1 teaspoon soft brown sugar

1 Cut the lasagne sheets into 15 even-sized pieces and trim lengthways so that they will fit neatly into a rectangular ovenproof dish when filled. Bring a large pan of water to a rapid boil. Cook 1–2 lasagne sheets at a time until just softened. This amount of time will differ depending on the type and brand of lasagne, but is usually about 2 minutes. Remove sheets carefully with two spatulas or wooden spoons and lay out flat on a clean damp tea towel. Do not use tongs to remove the sheets from the water as they might tear the sheets.
2 Heat the oil in a heavy-based frying pan. Cook the onion and garlic until golden, stirring regularly. Add the spinach and cook for 2 minutes, then cover with a tight-fitting lid and let the spinach steam for 5 minutes. Drain, removing as much liquid as possible. The spinach must be quite dry or the pasta will be soggy. Combine the spinach with the ricotta, eggs, nutmeg and season with salt and pepper. Mix well and set aside.
3 To make the tomato sauce, heat the oil in a frying pan and cook the onion and garlic for 10 minutes over low heat, stirring occasionally. Add the chopped tomatoes and their juice, tomato paste, sugar and 1/2 cup (125 ml/4 fl oz) water and season with salt and pepper. Bring the sauce to the boil, reduce the heat and simmer for 10 minutes. If you prefer a smooth sauce, purée it in a processor.
4 Preheat the oven to moderate 180°C (350°F/Gas 4) and lightly grease the ovenproof dish. Spread about one-third of the tomato sauce over the base of the dish. Working with one piece of the lasagne at a time, spoon 2½ table-spoons of the spinach mixture down the centre of each sheet, leaving a border at each end. Roll up and lay seam-side-down in the dish. Trim the ends to fit evenly if necessary. Spoon the remaining tomato sauce over the cannelloni and scatter the cheese over the top. Bake for 30–35 minutes, or until golden. Set aside for 10 minutes before serving.

NUTRITION PER SERVE
Protein 28 g; Fat 30 g; Carbohydrate 50 g;
Dietary Fibre 5 g; Cholesterol 128 mg;
2400 kJ (575 cal)

NOTE: You can use dried cannelloni tubes instead of fresh lasagne sheets. The texture of the pasta will be firmer.

NOODLES WITH BARBECUED PORK AND GREENS

Preparation time: 20 minutes
Total cooking time: 25 minutes
Serves 4

250 g (8 oz) fresh thick egg noodles
1 tablespoon oil
1 tablespoon sesame oil
250 g (8 oz) Chinese barbecued pork, cut into small cubes
1 large onion, very thinly sliced
2 cloves garlic, finely chopped
400 g (13 oz) green vegetables (beans, broccoli, celery), cut into bite-sized pieces
2 tablespoons hoisin sauce
1 tablespoon kecap manis
100 g (3½ oz) snow peas
3 baby bok choy, cut into quarters lengthways
230 g (7½ oz) can water chestnuts, sliced

1 Two-thirds fill a pan with water and bring to the boil. Add the noodles and cook for about 3 minutes, or until just tender. Drain well.
2 Heat the wok until very hot, add the oils and swirl them around to coat the side. Stir-fry the pork over medium heat for 2 minutes, or until crisp. Drain on paper towels.
3 Reheat the wok, add the onion and garlic, and stir-fry over very high heat for about 1 minute, or until just softened. Add the vegetables and cook, tossing regularly, for 2 minutes, or until just softened. Stir in the hoisin sauce, kecap manis, snow peas, bok choy, water chestnuts and 1 tablespoon of water. Cook for 2 minutes, covered. Add the noodles and stir-fried pork, and toss gently to combine. Serve immediately.

NUTRITION PER SERVE
Protein 10 g; Fat 20 g; Carbohydrate 60 g; Dietary Fibre 10 g; Cholesterol 40 mg; 3910 kJ (930 cal)

NOTE: Chinese barbecued pork is also known as *char siew*. You can buy it at Chinese barbecue shops.

Cut the barbecued pork into strips, then into small cubes.

Trim the base of the baby bok choy, then cut them into quarters lengthways.

Drain the can of water chestnuts and then slice them thinly.

CHICKEN AND VEGETABLE LASAGNE

Preparation time: 45 minutes
Total cooking time: 1 hour 20 minutes
Serves 8

500 g (1 lb) chicken breast fillets
cooking oil spray
2 cloves garlic, crushed
1 onion, chopped
2 zucchini, chopped
2 celery sticks, chopped
2 carrots, chopped
300 g (10 oz) pumpkin, diced
2 x 400 g (13 oz) cans tomatoes,
    chopped
2 fresh thyme sprigs
2 bay leaves
1/2 cup (125 ml/4 fl oz) white wine
2 tablespoons tomato paste
2 tablespoons chopped fresh basil
500 g (1 lb) English spinach
500 g (1 lb) reduced-fat cottage
    cheese
450 g (14 oz) ricotta
1/4 cup (60 ml/2 fl oz) skim milk
1/2 teaspoon ground nutmeg
1/3 cup (35 g/11/4 oz) grated
    Parmesan
300 g (10 oz) instant or fresh lasagne
    sheets

1 Preheat the oven to moderate 180°C (350°F/Gas 4). Trim excess fat from the chicken breasts, then finely mince in a food processor. Heat a large, deep, non-stick frying pan, spray lightly with oil and cook the chicken mince in batches until browned. Remove and set aside.

2 Add the garlic and onion to the pan and cook until softened. Return the chicken to the pan and add the zucchini, celery, carrot, pumpkin, tomato, thyme, bay leaves, wine and tomato paste. Simmer, covered, for 20 minutes. Remove the bay leaves and thyme, stir in the fresh basil and set aside.

3 Shred the spinach and set aside. Mix the cottage cheese, ricotta, skim milk, nutmeg and half the Parmesan.

4 Spoon a little of the tomato mixture over the base of a casserole dish and top with a single layer of pasta. Top with half the remaining tomato mixture, then the spinach and spoon over half the cottage cheese mixture. Continue with another layer of pasta, the remaining tomato and another layer of pasta. Spread the remaining cottage cheese mixture on top and sprinkle with Parmesan. Bake for 40–50 minutes, or until golden. The top may puff up slightly but will settle on standing.

NUTRITION PER SERVE
Protein 40 g; Fat 10 g; Carbohydrate 35 g;
Dietary Fibre 7 g; Cholesterol 70 mg;
1790 kJ (430 cal)

Finely mince the trimmed chicken breast fillets in a food processor.

Add the vegetables with the thyme, bay leaves, wine and tomato paste to the pan.

BLACK BEAN BEEF WITH NOODLES

Preparation time: 15 minutes
Total cooking time: 10 minutes
Serves 4

250 g (8 oz) instant noodles
500 g (1 lb) beef, thinly sliced
2 teaspoons sesame oil
2 cloves garlic, crushed
1 tablespoon grated fresh ginger
oil, for cooking
6 spring onions, sliced on the diagonal
1 small red capsicum, thinly sliced
125 g (4 oz) snow peas, halved on the diagonal

4 tablespoons black bean and garlic sauce (see NOTE)
2 tablespoons hoisin sauce
1/2 cup (60 g/2 oz) bean sprouts

1 Cook the noodles according to the manufacturer's directions, then drain and keep warm.
2 Place the beef, sesame oil, garlic and ginger in a bowl and mix together well. Heat the wok until very hot, add 1 tablespoon of the oil and swirl it around to coat the side. Add half the beef and stir-fry for 2–3 minutes, or until the beef is just cooked. Remove from the wok, add a little more oil and cook the rest of the beef. Remove all the beef from the wok.

3 Heat 1 tablespoon oil in the wok. Add the spring onion, capsicum and snow peas and stir-fry for 2 minutes. Return the beef to the wok and stir in the black bean and garlic sauce, hoisin sauce and 1 tablespoon water.
4 Add the noodles to the wok and toss to heat through. Serve immediately, topped with bean sprouts.

NUTRITION PER SERVE
Protein 30 g; Fat 20 g; Carbohydrate 25 g; Dietary Fibre 5.7 g; Cholesterol 76 mg; 1751 kJ (418 cal)

NOTE: Black bean and garlic sauce is available at Asian grocery stores or good supermarkets.

Add the beef and marinade to the wok and stir-fry in two batches over high heat.

Stir-fry the spring onion, capsicum and snow peas for 2 minutes.

Add the noodles and stir to coat with the beef and vegetables.

SPEEDY CHICKEN AND PASTA BAKE

Preparation time: 15 minutes
Total cooking time: 45 minutes
Serves 4

200 g (6¹/₂ oz) spiral pasta
425 g (14 oz) can cream of mushroom or broccoli soup
1 cup (250 g/8 oz) sour cream
1 teaspoon curry powder
1 barbecued chicken
250 g (8 oz) broccoli, cut into small pieces
1 cup (90 g/3 oz) fresh breadcrumbs
1¹/₂ cups (185 g/6 oz) grated Cheddar

1 Preheat the oven to moderate 180°C (350°F/Gas 4). Cook the pasta in a large pan of rapidly boiling salted water until *al dente*. Drain and return to the pan to keep warm.
2 Combine the soup, sour cream and curry powder and season to taste with freshly ground black pepper.
3 Remove the meat from the chicken and roughly chop. Combine the chicken with the pasta, broccoli and soup mixture. Spoon into four lightly greased 2-cup (500 ml/16 fl oz) ovenproof dishes and sprinkle with the combined breadcrumbs and cheese. Bake for 25–30 minutes, or until the cheese melts.

NUTRITION PER SERVE
Protein 67 g; Fat 47 g; Carbohydrate 55 g; Dietary Fibre 8 g; Cholesterol 254 mg; 3812 kJ (911 cal)

VARIATION: This recipe can be made in a 2-litre ovenproof dish and baked for 40 minutes, or until the cheese has melted.

Cook the pasta in a large pan of rapidly boiling water until it is tender.

Mix together the soup, sour cream and curry powder to make the sauce.

Mix together the chicken meat, pasta, broccoli and sauce.

CHICKEN AND PUMPKIN CANNELLONI

Preparation time: 1 hour
Total cooking time: 2 hours
Serves 6

500 g (1 lb) butternut pumpkin, with skin and seeds
30 g (1 oz) butter
100 g (3$^{1}/_{2}$ oz) pancetta, roughly chopped
2 teaspoons olive oil
2 cloves garlic, crushed
500 g (1 lb) chicken thigh fillets, minced
$^{1}/_{2}$ teaspoon garam masala
2 tablespoons chopped fresh flat-leaf parsley
150 g (5 oz) goats cheese
50 g (1$^{3}/_{4}$ oz) ricotta
375 g (12 oz) fresh lasagne sheets
1 cup (100 g/3$^{1}/_{2}$ oz) grated Parmesan

TOMATO SAUCE
30 g (1 oz) butter
1 clove garlic, crushed
2 x 425 g (14 oz) cans chopped tomatoes
$^{1}/_{4}$ cup (7 g/$^{1}/_{4}$ oz) chopped fresh flat-leaf parsley
$^{1}/_{4}$ cup (60 ml/2 fl oz) white wine

1 Preheat the oven to hot 220°C (425°F/Gas 7). Brush the pumpkin with 10 g ($^{1}/_{4}$ oz) of the butter and bake on a baking tray for 1 hour, or until tender. When the pumpkin has cooked and while it is still hot, remove the seeds. Scrape out the flesh and mash it with a fork. Set aside to cool.
2 Add another 10 g ($^{1}/_{4}$ oz) of the butter to a heavy-based frying pan and cook the pancetta over medium heat for 2–3 minutes. Remove from the pan and drain on paper towels.

3 In the same pan, heat the remaining butter and the olive oil. Add the garlic and stir for 30 seconds. Add the chicken in small batches and brown, making sure the chicken is cooked through. Remove from the pan and set aside to cool on paper towels. Reduce the oven temperature to moderately hot 200°C (400°F/Gas 6).
4 Combine the pumpkin with the pancetta and chicken in a bowl. Mix in the garam marsala, parsley, goats cheese, ricotta and some salt and black pepper. Cut the lasagne sheets into rough 15 cm (6 inch) squares. Place 3 tablespoons of the filling at one end of each square and roll up. Repeat with the rest of the lasagne sheets and filling.
5 To make the tomato sauce, melt the butter in a heavy-based pan and add the garlic. Cook for 1 minute, then add the tomato and simmer over medium heat for 1 minute. Add the parsley and white wine, and simmer gently for another 5 minutes. Season with salt and pepper, to taste.
6 Spread a little of the tomato sauce over the bottom of a 3 litre capacity ovenproof dish and arrange the cannelloni on top in a single layer. Spoon the remaining tomato sauce over the cannelloni and sprinkle with the Parmesan. Bake for 20–25 minutes, or until the cheese is golden.

NUTRITION PER SERVE
Protein 44 g; Fat 26 g; Carbohydrate 55 g; Dietary Fibre 6.5 g; Cholesterol 113 mg; 2670 kJ (638 cal)

NOTE: You can use instant cannelloni tubes instead of the lasagne sheets. Stand the tubes on end on a chopping board and spoon in the filling.

Roughly chop the pancetta slices with a large cook's knife.

Finely mince the chicken thigh fillets using a food processor.

Scrape out the flesh of the cooked pumpkin and mash with a fork.

Combine the pumpkin, pancetta, chicken and other filling ingredients in a bowl.

Place 3 tablespoons of the filling onto the end of each lasagne sheet and roll up.

Arrange the cannelloni tubes over a little of the tomato sauce in the dish.

grills & fries

BRUNCH BURGER WITH THE WORKS

Preparation time: 40 minutes
Total cooking time: 15 minutes
Serves 6

750 g (1¹/₂ lb) lean beef mince
1 onion, finely chopped
1 egg
¹/₂ cup (40 g/1¹/₄ oz) fresh
    breadcrumbs
2 tablespoons tomato paste
1 tablespoon Worcestershire sauce
2 tablespoons chopped fresh parsley
3 large onions
30 g (1 oz) butter
6 slices Cheddar cheese
6 eggs, extra
6 rashers bacon
6 large hamburger buns, lightly
    toasted
shredded lettuce
2 tomatoes, thinly sliced
6 large slices beetroot, drained
6 pineapple rings, drained
tomato sauce

1 Mix together the mince, onion, egg, breadcrumbs, tomato paste, Worcestershire sauce and parsley with your hands. Season well. Divide into six portions and shape into burgers. Cover and set aside.
2 Slice the onions into thin rings. Heat the butter on a barbecue grill. Cook the onions, turning often, until well browned. Move the onions to the outer edge of the grill to keep warm. Brush the barbecue grill liberally with oil.
3 Cook the burgers for 3–4 minutes each side or until browned and cooked through. Move to the cooler part of the barbecue or transfer to plate and keep warm. Place a slice of cheese on each burger.
4 Heat a small amount of butter in a large frying pan. Fry the eggs and bacon until the eggs are cooked through and the bacon is golden and crisp. Fill the hamburger buns with lettuce, tomato, beetroot and pineapple topped with a burger. Pile the onions, egg, bacon and tomato sauce on top of the burger.

NUTRITION PER SERVE
Protein 35 g; Fat 23 g; Carbohydrate 11 g;
Dietary Fibre 2 g; Cholesterol 300 mg;
1610 kJ (385 cal)

Mix together the mince, onion, egg, bread-crumbs, tomato paste, sauce and parsley.

Divide the meat mixture into six portions and shape each one into a burger.

Cook the burgers on a barbecue grill or flatplate for 3–4 minutes on each side.

GRILLED CHICKEN SKEWERS

Preparation time: 20 minutes +
  2 hours marinating
Total cooking time: 10 minutes
Serves 4

32 chicken tenderloins
24 (180 g/6 oz) cherry tomatoes
6 cap mushrooms, cut into quarters
2 cloves garlic, crushed
rind of 1 lemon, grated
2 tablespoons lemon juice
1 tablespoon olive oil
1 tablespoon fresh oregano leaves, chopped

1 Soak 8 wooden skewers for at least 30 minutes to prevent burning. Thread a piece of chicken onto each skewer, followed by a tomato, then a piece of mushroom. Repeat three times for each skewer.
2 Combine the garlic, lemon rind, lemon juice, olive oil and chopped oregano, pour over the skewers and toss well. Marinate for at least 2 hours.
3 Place the skewers on a barbecue grill and cook under high heat for 5 minutes each side, basting while cooking, or until the chicken is cooked and the tomatoes have shrivelled slightly. Serve hot with a green salad.

NUTRITION PER SERVE
Protein 34 g; Fat 8 g; Carbohydrate 1 g;
Dietary Fibre 1 g; Cholesterol 75 mg;
909 kJ (217 cal)

NOTE: The skewers can be made in advance and marinated for up to a day before cooking.

Thread the chicken, tomato and mushrooms onto the skewers.

Leave the skewers in the marinade for at least 2 hours and overnight if possible.

Grill the skewers, basting with the marinade as they cook.

SAUSAGES AND MASH WITH ONION GRAVY

Preparation time: 10 minutes
Total cooking time: 50 minutes
Serves 4

1½ cups (375 ml/12 fl oz) beef stock
2 teaspoons cornflour
2 teaspoons balsamic vinegar
1 tablespoon oil
6 onions, sliced
1.5 kg (3 lb) potatoes, chopped
60 g (2 oz) butter
½ cup (125 ml/4 fl oz) cream
8 beef sausages

1 Mix together 1 tablespoon stock with the cornflour, and stir to dissolve, ensuring there are no lumps. Add to the remaining stock with the vinegar.
2 To make the onion gravy, heat the oil in a large frying pan, add the onion and cook over low heat for 35–40 minutes, or until the onion is soft and beginning to caramelise.

Increase the heat and slowly add the stock mixture, stirring constantly until the mixture thickens. Remove from the heat and set aside.
3 Meanwhile, put the potatoes in a large pan of boiling water and cook for 15–20 minutes, or until tender. Drain the potatoes and return them to the pan with the butter and cream. With a potato masher, mash until smooth and creamy. Season to taste with salt and cracked black pepper.
4 Prick the sausages and cook under a hot grill (broiler), turning

once, for 10 minutes, or until cooked through.
5 Gently warm the gravy and serve with sausages and mashed potato. Delicious with baked zucchini.

NUTRITION PER SERVE
Protein 30 g; Fat 70 g; Carbohydrate 63 g; Dietary Fibre 13 g; Cholesterol 160 mg; 4280 kJ (1025 Cal)

NOTE: The gravy can be warmed in the microwave just before serving.

Cook the onion in the oil until soft and beginning to caramelise.

Slowly pour in the stock mixture and stir constantly until the gravy thickens.

STUFFED CHICKEN BREASTS

Preparation time: 40 minutes
Total cooking time: 45 minutes
Serves 6

1 tablespoon olive oil
1 onion, finely chopped
2 cloves garlic, crushed
100 g (3¹/₂ oz) ham, finely chopped
1 green capsicum, finely chopped
2 tablespoons finely chopped pitted
    black olives
¹/₃ cup (35 g/1¹/₄ oz) grated
    Parmesan
6 chicken breast fillets

plain flour, to coat
2 eggs, lightly beaten
1¹/₂ cups (150 g/5 oz) dry
    breadcrumbs
¹/₄ cup (60 ml/2 fl oz) olive oil

1 Heat the oil in a pan and add the onion, garlic, ham and capsicum. Cook, stirring, over medium heat for 5 minutes, or until the onion is soft. Remove and place in a heatproof bowl. Add the olives and Parmesan.
2 Cut a deep pocket in the side of each chicken fillet, cutting almost through to the other side.
3 Fill each fillet with the ham mixture and secure with toothpicks along the opening of the pocket. Coat each fillet

with the flour, shaking off any excess. Dip into the beaten egg and then coat with the breadcrumbs. Heat the oil in a large pan and cook the fillets, in batches, over medium-high heat for 15–20 minutes, turning halfway through, until golden and cooked through. To serve, remove the toothpicks, then cut diagonally into thin slices.

NUTRITION PER SERVE
Protein 35 g; Fat 20 g; Carbohydrate 20 g;
Dietary Fibre 2 g; Cholesterol 115 mg;
1660 kJ (395 cal)

Cut a deep pocket in the side of each fillet, cutting almost through to the other side.

Spoon the filling into each fillet, securing the pocket openings with toothpicks.

Coat the chicken breasts in the beaten egg and breadcrumbs before cooking.

GRILLED LAMB PITTAS WITH FRESH MINT SALAD

Preparation time: 20 minutes +
    30 minutes refrigeration
Total cooking time: 15 minutes
Serves 4

1 kg (2 lb) lean minced lamb
1 cup (60 g/2 oz) finely chopped fresh
    flat-leaf parsley
1/2 cup (25 g/3/4 oz) finely chopped
    fresh mint
1 onion, finely chopped
1 clove garlic, crushed
1 egg
1 teaspoon chilli sauce
4 small wholemeal pitta pockets

MINT SALAD
3 small vine-ripened tomatoes
1 small red onion, finely sliced
1 cup (20 g/3/4 oz) fresh mint
1 tablespoon olive oil
2 tablespoons lemon juice

1 Place the lamb, parsley, mint, onion,
garlic, egg and chilli sauce in a large
bowl and mix together well. Shape
into eight small patties. Chill for
30 minutes. Preheat the oven to
warm 160°C (315°F/Gas 2–3).
2 To make the mint salad, slice the
tomatoes into thin rings and place
in a bowl with the onion, mint, olive
oil and lemon juice. Season well with
salt and freshly ground black pepper.
Gently toss to coat.

3 Wrap the pitta breads in foil and
warm in the oven for 5–10 minutes.
4 Heat a chargrill or barbecue hot
plate and brush with a little oil.
When very hot, cook the patties for
3 minutes on each side. Do not turn
until a nice crust has formed on the
base or they will fall apart when you
move them.
5 Remove the pitta breads from the
oven. Cut the pockets in half, fill each
half with some mint salad and a lamb
patty. Serve with some low-fat
yoghurt, if desired.

NUTRITION PER SERVE
Protein 59 g; Fat 24 g; Carbohydrate 29 g;
Dietary Fibre 8 g; Cholesterol 211 mg; 2390 kJ
(570 Cal)

Mix the lamb, herbs, onion, garlic, egg and chilli
sauce together with your hands.

Toss together the tomato and onion slices, mint,
oil and lemon juice.

Chargrill the patties on a lightly oiled surface until
a crust has formed.

CHICKEN KEBABS WITH CURRY MAYONNAISE

Preparation time: 25 minutes
  + 30 minutes marinating
Total cooking time: 10 minutes
Serves 4

600 g (1¼ lb) chicken breast fillets
4 large spring onions
1 small green capsicum
1 small red capsicum
¼ cup (60 ml/2 fl oz) olive oil
1 teaspoon freshly ground black
  pepper
½ teaspoon ground turmeric
1½ teaspoons ground coriander

CURRY MAYONNAISE
¾ cup (185 g/6 oz) whole-egg
  mayonnaise
1 tablespoon hot curry powder
¼ cup (60 g/2 oz) sour cream
1 tablespoon sweet fruit or mango
  chutney, mashed
¼ cup (45 g/1½ oz) peeled, finely
  chopped cucumber
½ teaspoon toasted cumin seeds
1 tablespoon finely chopped fresh
  mint
1 teaspoon finely chopped fresh mint,
  extra

1 Preheat a barbecue grill or flatplate to high. Trim the chicken of excess fat and sinew. Cut the chicken into 3 cm (1¼ inch) cubes. Cut the spring onions into 3 cm (1¼ inch) lengths. Cut the green and red capsicum into 3 cm (1¼ inch) squares.
2 Thread the chicken, spring onion and capsicum onto skewers. Arrange the kebabs, side by side, in a shallow, non-metal dish. Combine the oil, pepper, turmeric and coriander in a jug. Pour over the kebabs and place in the refrigerator to marinate for 30 minutes.
3 To make the curry mayonnaise, combine the mayonnaise, curry powder, sour cream, chutney, cucumber, cumin seeds and mint in a bowl, and mix well. Spoon the mixture into a dish or jug for serving and sprinkle with the extra chopped mint.
4 Lightly oil the hot barbecue grill or flatplate. Cook the kebabs for 2–3 minutes each side, or until cooked through and tender. Serve with the curry mayonnaise.

NUTRITION PER SERVE
Protein 36 g; Fat 40 g; Carbohydrate 14 g; Dietary Fibre 2 g; Cholesterol 110 mg; 2316 kJ (553 Cal)

Cut the chicken, spring onions and capsicums into even-sized pieces.

Pour the oil mixture over the chicken kebabs, and marinate for 30 minutes.

Combine the curry mayonnaise ingredients in a bowl and mix well.

SWEET AND SOUR PORK

Preparation time: 25 minutes
  + 30 minutes marinating
Total cooking time: 20 minutes
Serves 4

500 g (1 lb) pork fillet, thickly sliced
2 tablespoons cornflour
1 tablespoon sherry
1 tablespoon soy sauce
1 tablespoon sugar
oil, for cooking
1 large onion, thinly sliced
1 green capsicum, cut into cubes
2 small carrots, thinly sliced
1 small Lebanese cucumber, seeded
  and chopped
5 spring onions, cut into short lengths
440 g (14 oz) can pineapple pieces in
  juice, drained, juice reserved
1/4 cup (60 ml/2 fl oz) white vinegar
1/2 teaspoon salt

1 Place the pork in a shallow glass or ceramic bowl. Combine the cornflour with the sherry, soy sauce and half the sugar and add to the pork. Cover and refrigerate for 30 minutes.
2 Drain the pork, reserving the marinade. Heat the wok until very hot, add 1 tablespoon of oil and swirl to coat the side. Stir-fry half the pork over high heat for 4–5 minutes, or until the pork is golden brown and just cooked. Remove from the wok and cook the remaining pork, adding a little more oil if necessary. Remove all the pork from the wok.
3 Reheat the wok, add 1 tablespoon of oil and stir-fry the onion over high heat for 3–4 minutes, or until slightly softened. Add the capsicum and carrot, and cook for 3–4 minutes, or until tender. Stir in the marinade,

cucumber, spring onion, pineapple, vinegar, salt, remaining sugar and 4 tablespoons of the reserved pineapple juice.
4 Bring to the boil and simmer for 2–3 minutes, or until the sauce has thickened slightly. Return the pork to the wok and toss until the pork is heated through. Serve immediately with steamed rice.

NUTRITION PER SERVE
Protein 25 g; Fat 12 g; Carbohydrate 25 g;
Dietary Fibre 4 g; Cholesterol 50 mg;
1325 kJ (315 cal)

Peel the carrots, if necessary, and cut them into thin diagonal slices.

Halve the cucumber lengthways and scoop out the seeds with a teaspoon.

Stir-fry the pork until it is golden brown and just cooked through.

CHICKEN BURGER WITH TANGY GARLIC MAYONNAISE

Preparation time: 20 minutes
  + 3 hours marinating
Total cooking time: 15 minutes
Serves 4

4 chicken breast fillets
1/2 cup (125 ml/4 fl oz) lime juice
1 tablespoon sweet chilli sauce
4 slices bacon
4 hamburger buns, halved
4 lettuce leaves
1 large tomato, sliced

GARLIC MAYONNAISE
2 egg yolks
2 cloves garlic, crushed
1 tablespoon Dijon mustard
1 tablespoon lemon juice
1/2 cup (125 ml/4 fl oz) olive oil

1 Place the chicken in a shallow non-metal dish. Prick the chicken breasts with a skewer several times. Combine the lime juice and sweet chilli sauce in a jug. Pour the mixture over the chicken, cover and refrigerate for several hours or overnight.
2 To make the mayonnaise, place the egg yolks, garlic, mustard and lemon juice in a food processor bowl or blender and process until smooth. With the motor running, add the oil in a thin, steady stream. Process until the mixture reaches a thick consistency. Refrigerate, covered, until required.
3 Preheat a barbecue grill or flatplate to high. Remove and discard the rind from the bacon, and cut the bacon in half crossways. Lightly grease the hot barbecue. Cook the chicken and bacon for 5 minutes, or until crisp. Cook the chicken for a further 5–10 minutes, or until well browned and cooked through, turning once.
4 Toast the hamburger buns until lightly browned. Arrange the lettuce, tomato, chicken and bacon on the bases. Top with the garlic mayonnaise and finish with the remaining bun top.

NUTRITION PER SERVE
Protein 70 g; Fat 42 g; Carbohydrate 52 g; Dietary Fibre 5 g; Cholesterol 211 mg; 3624 kJ (866 cal)

VARIATION: For a tangy mayonnaise, substitute the lemon juice with lime juice and omit the garlic.

Pour the combined lime juice and sweet chilli sauce over the chicken fillets.

Cook the chicken until it is well browned and cooked through, turning once.

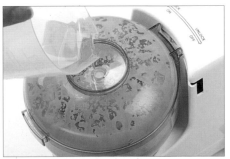

Add the oil to the egg yolk mixture in a thin, steady stream.

FILLET STEAK WITH ONION MARMALADE

Preparation time: 20 minutes
Total cooking time: 1 hour
Serves 4

4 thick rib-eye steaks
30 g (1 oz) butter
2 red onions, thinly sliced
2 tablespoons soft brown sugar
1 tablespoon balsamic vinegar

1 Trim any fat from the steaks, then sprinkle liberally with freshly ground black pepper. Cover and refrigerate until ready to cook.
2 To make the onion marmalade, heat the butter in a heavy-based pan. Add the onion and cook, stirring often, for 10 minutes over low heat, or until the onion is soft but not brown. Stir in the brown sugar and balsamic vinegar and continue to cook for about 30 minutes, stirring frequently. The mixture will become thick and glossy.

3 Place the steaks on a hot, lightly oiled barbecue grill or flatplate and cook for 3 minutes each side to seal, turning once only. For rare steaks, cook a further minute. For medium, cook for another few minutes and for well done, about 5 minutes. Serve at once with the onion marmalade.

NUTRITION PER SERVE
Protein 30 g; Fat 10 g; Carbohydrate 25 g;
Dietary Fibre 4 g; Cholesterol 100 mg;
1355 kJ (320 cal)

Trim any fat from the steaks and then sprinkle liberally with black pepper.

Cook the onion marmalade for about 30 minutes, or until it is thick and glossy.

Cook the steaks for 3 minutes on each side to seal them, then cook to your taste.

FISH AND CHIPS

Preparation time: 25 minutes + soaking
Total cooking time: 30 minutes
Serves 4

1¼ cups (155 g/5 oz) plain flour
1½ cups (375 ml/12 fl oz) beer
4 floury potatoes (e.g. spunta, russet or King Edward)
oil, for deep-frying
4 firm white fish fillets
cornflour, for coating
lemon wedges, for serving

1 Sift the flour into a large bowl, make a well and gradually add the beer, whisking to make a smooth lump-free batter. Cover and set aside. Preheat the oven to moderate 180°C (350°F/Gas 4).

2 Cut the potatoes into 1 cm (³⁄₄ inch) thick chips. Soak in cold water for 10 minutes, drain and pat dry. Fill a deep heavy-based saucepan one-third full of oil and heat to 160°C (315°F), or until a cube of bread browns in 30 seconds. Cook batches of chips for 4–5 minutes, or until pale golden. Remove with a slotted spoon. Drain on crumpled paper towels.

3 Just before serving, reheat the oil to moderate 180°C (350°F), or until a cube of bread browns in 15 seconds. Cook the chips again, in batches, until crisp and golden. Drain. Keep hot on a baking tray in the oven.

4 Pat the fish dry with paper towels. Dust with cornflour, dip into the batter and drain off any excess. Deep-fry in batches for 5–7 minutes, or until cooked through. Turn with tongs if necessary. Remove with a slotted spoon and drain on crumpled paper towels. Serve with chips and lemon.

NUTRITION PER SERVE
Protein 22.5 g; Fat 18 g; Carbohydrate 51.5 g; Dietary Fibre 4 g; Cholesterol 49 mg; 2035 kJ (485 Cal)

SUGGESTED FISH: Fillets of bream, cod, coley, flake, flathead, pollack or snapper.

Whisk the flour and beer together until you have a smooth lump-free batter.

Cut the peeled potatoes into thick even-sized chips.

Cook the chips in batches a second time until crisp and golden.

If you need to turn the fish over during cooking, use tongs to handle.

CHICKEN CORDON BLEU

Preparation time: 15 minutes
  + 30 minutes refrigeration
Total cooking time: 20 minutes
Serves 4

4 (460 g/14 oz) chicken
    breast fillets
4 thick slices Swiss cheese
4 slices double-smoked ham or
    pastrami
$1/3$ cup (40 g/$1^{1}/4$ oz) seasoned plain
    flour
1 egg, lightly beaten
$1/2$ cup (50 g/$1^{3}/4$ oz) dry
    breadcrumbs
$1/2$ cup (125 ml/4 fl oz) oil

1 Trim the chicken of excess fat and
sinew. Using a sharp knife, cut into the
thickest section of each fillet without
cutting right through. Open the fillet
out flat and season with salt and
freshly ground black pepper.
2 Place a slice of cheese and ham on
one side of each fillet. Fold the
remaining half of the fillet over to
enclose the filling.
3 Carefully coat each fillet with flour,
then shake off the excess. Dip into
the egg, then coat with the
breadcrumbs. Place on a foil-lined
baking tray. Place, covered, in the
refrigerator for 30 minutes.
4 Heat the oil in a medium heavy-
based pan. Add the chicken and cook
in two batches over medium heat for
4 minutes each side, or until the
chicken is golden and cooked
through. Add more oil between
batches if necessary. Serve the
chicken immediately.

NUTRITION PER SERVE
Protein 40 g; Fat 40 g; Carbohydrate 16 g;
Dietary Fibre 1 g; Cholesterol 130 mg;
2438 kJ (582 cal)

Cut into the thickest section of each chicken fillet
without cutting right through.

Place a slice of cheese and a slice of ham on
one side of each fillet.

Shake the excess flour from the chicken, then dip
into the beaten egg.

Cook the chicken in the oil for 4 minutes each
side, or until golden and cooked through.

BEEF SATAY STICKS WITH PEANUT SAUCE

Preparation time: 30 minutes +
  at least 3 hours marinating
Total cooking time: 15 minutes
Serves 4

800 g (1 lb 10 oz) rump steak
1/3 cup (80 ml/2³/₄ fl oz) soy sauce
2 tablespoons oil
2 cloves garlic, crushed
1 teaspoon grated fresh ginger

PEANUT SAUCE
1 cup (250 ml/8 fl oz) pineapple juice
1 cup (250 g/8 oz) peanut butter
1/2 teaspoon garlic powder
1/2 teaspoon onion powder
2 tablespoons sweet chilli sauce
3 tablespoons soy sauce

1 Trim the steak of excess fat and sinew. Slice across the grain evenly into long, thin strips. Thread onto skewers, bunching them thickly along three-quarters of the skewer. Place in a shallow non-metal dish.
2 Mix the soy sauce, oil, garlic and ginger together and pour over the satays. Cover with plastic wrap and refrigerate for several hours or overnight, turning occasionally.
3 Cook on a hot, lightly oiled barbecue grill or flatplate for 8–10 minutes or until tender, turning the skewers occasionally.

4 To make the peanut sauce, combine the juice, peanut butter, garlic and onion powders and sauces in a small pan and stir over medium heat for 5 minutes or until smooth. Serve warm with the satay sticks.

NUTRITION PER SERVE
Protein 70 g; Fat 55 g; Carbohydrate 17 g; Dietary Fibre 9 g; Cholesterol 134 mg; 3500 kJ (838 cal)

STORAGE: The sauce can be made a day in advance and stored in the fridge. If it thickens too much on standing, add a little warm water when reheating.

Trim the meat and then slice across the grain into long, thin strips.

Thread the meat onto skewers and then leave to marinate in a non-metallic dish.

To make the peanut sauce, stir all the ingredients over medium heat until smooth.

MEDITERRANEAN BURGERS

Preparation time: 15 minutes
Total cooking time: 20 minutes
Serves 4

1 large red capsicum
500 g (1 lb) lamb mince
1 egg, lightly beaten
1 small onion, grated
3 cloves garlic, crushed
2 tablespoons pine nuts, chopped
1 tablespoon finely chopped fresh
    mint
1 tablespoon finely chopped fresh
    parsley
1 teaspoon ground cumin
2 teaspoons chilli sauce
1 tablespoon olive oil
4 Turkish or pide bread rolls
1 cup (220 g/7 oz) ready-made
    hummus
100 g (3½ oz) baby rocket
1 small Lebanese cucumber,
    cut into ribbons
chilli sauce, to serve (optional)

1 Cut the capsicum into large pieces, removing the seeds and membrane. Place, skin-side-up, under a hot grill (broiler) until the skin blackens and blisters. Cool in a plastic bag, then peel and cut into thick strips.
2 Combine the mince, egg, onion, garlic, pine nuts, fresh herbs, cumin and chilli sauce in a large bowl. Mix with your hands and roll into four even-sized balls. Press the balls into large patties about 9 cm (3½ inches) in diameter.
3 Heat the oil in a large frying pan and cook the patties over medium heat for 6 minutes each side, or until well browned and cooked through, then drain on paper towels.
4 Halve the rolls and toast both sides.
5 Spread the cut sides of the rolls with hummus, then lay rocket leaves, roasted capsicum and cucumber ribbons over the base. Place a patty on the salad and top with the other half of the roll. Serve with chilli sauce.

NUTRITION PER SERVE
Protein 40 g; Fat 30 g; Carbohydrate 54 g;
Dietary Fibre 7 g; Cholesterol 124 mg;
2758 kJ (660 Cal)

Cook the capsicum under a hot grill until the skin blackens and blisters.

Roll the mince mixture into even-sized balls and then flatten into patties.

CHICKEN MARSALA

Preparation time: 10 minutes
Total cooking time: 25 minutes
Serves 4

4 chicken breast fillets
2 tablespoons oil
60 g (2 oz) butter
1 clove garlic, crushed
2 cups (500 ml/16 fl oz) chicken
    stock
1/3 cup (80 ml/2³/4 fl oz) Marsala
2 teaspoons plain flour
2 teaspoons Worcestershire
    sauce
1/4 cup (60 ml/2 fl oz) cream

1 Trim the chicken of excess fat and sinew. Heat the oil in a heavy-based frying pan and add the chicken. Cook over medium heat for 4 minutes on each side, or until cooked through and lightly golden. Remove the chicken, cover loosely with foil and keep warm. Drain off any fat from the pan.
2 Add the butter and garlic to the pan and stir over medium heat for 2 minutes. Add the combined stock and Marsala and bring to the boil. Reduce the heat and simmer for 10 minutes, or until the liquid has reduced by half.
3 Stir the flour, Worcestershire sauce and cream together. Add a little of the hot liquid and blend to a paste. Add to the pan and stir over medium heat until the sauce boils and thickens. Season to taste and then pour over the chicken fillets. Delicious with pasta.

NUTRITION PER SERVE
Protein 55 g; Fat 35 g; Carbohydrate 2 g; Dietary Fibre 0 g; Cholesterol 180 mg; 2220 kJ (530 cal)

VARIATION: Marsala is a sweet wine and so makes a sweet-tasting sauce. Port or any dry red wine can be used instead. Boiling wine evaporates the alcohol, leaving the flavour but not the intoxicating qualities. Chicken thighs or drumsticks can be used instead of breast fillets.

Cook the chicken in a frying pan until lightly golden on each side.

Mix together the stock and Marsala, then add to the pan and bring to the boil.

Add the Worcestershire sauce mixture and stir over the heat until thickened.

ASIAN BARBECUED CHICKEN

Preparation time: 10 minutes +
　2 hours marinating
Total cooking time: 25 minutes
Serves 6

2 cloves garlic, finely chopped
1/4 cup (60 ml/2 fl oz) hoisin sauce
3 teaspoons light soy sauce
3 teaspoons honey
1 teaspoon sesame oil
2 tablespoons tomato sauce
　or sweet chilli sauce
2 spring onions, finely sliced
1.5 kg (3 lb) chicken wings

1 To make the marinade, combine the garlic, hoisin sauce, soy, honey, sesame oil, tomato sauce and spring onion in a small bowl.
2 Pour over the chicken wings, cover and marinate in the refrigerator for at least 2 hours.
3 Place the chicken on a barbecue grill and cook, in batches, turning once, for 20–25 minutes, or until cooked and golden brown. Baste with the marinade during cooking. Heat any remaining marinade in a pan until boiling and serve as a sauce.

NUTRITION PER SERVE
Protein 26 g; Fat 8.5 g; Carbohydrate 9 g;
Dietary Fibre 1.5 g; Cholesterol 111 mg;
916 kJ (219 cal)

NOTE: The chicken can also be baked in a moderate 180°C (350°F/Gas 4) oven for 30 minutes (turn once).

Mix together the garlic, hoisin, soy, honey, sesame oil, tomato sauce and spring onion.

Pour the marinade over the chicken wings and marinate in the fridge.

Cook the chicken wings in batches on a barbecue, or bake in the oven.

BACON-WRAPPED CHICKEN

Preparation time: 15 minutes
Total cooking time: 10 minutes
Serves 6

2 tablespoons olive oil
2 tablespoons lime juice
$1/4$ teaspoon ground coriander
6 chicken breast fillets
4 tablespoons fruit chutney
3 tablespoons chopped pecan nuts
6 slices bacon

1 Mix together the oil, lime juice, coriander and salt and pepper. Using a sharp knife, cut a pocket in the thickest section of each fillet. Mix together the chutney and nuts. Spoon 1 tablespoon of the chutney mixture into each chicken breast pocket.
2 Turn the tapered ends of the fillets to the underside. Wrap a bacon slice around each fillet to enclose the filling and secure with a toothpick.
3 Put the chicken parcels on a hot, lightly oiled barbecue grill or flatplate and cook for 5 minutes on each side, or until cooked through, turning once. Brush with the lime juice mixture several times during cooking and drizzle with any leftover lime juice mixture to serve.

NUTRITION PER SERVE
Protein 72 g; Fat 28 g; Carbohydrate 19 g; Dietary Fibre 1 g; Cholesterol 164 mg; 2589 kJ (618 cal)

VARIATION: This recipe also works well with prosciutto, which is an Italian equivalent of bacon.

Mix together the fruit chutney and pecans to make a filling for the chicken.

Wrap a piece of bacon around each breast and secure with a toothpick or skewer.

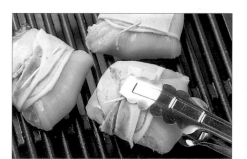

Cook the chicken on a hot barbecue grill for 5 minutes on each side.

Brush the chicken with the lime juice mixture during cooking.

TANGY BEEF RIBS

Preparation time: 20 minutes +
    3 hours marinating
Total cooking time: 15–20 minutes
Serves 4

1 kg (2 lb) beef ribs
1/2 cup (125 ml/4 fl oz) tomato sauce
2 tablespoons Worcestershire sauce
2 tablespoons soft brown sugar
1 teaspoon paprika
1/4 teaspoon chilli powder
1 clove garlic, crushed

1 Chop the ribs into individual serving pieces, if necessary (see NOTES). Bring a large pan of water to the boil. Cook the ribs in boiling water for 5 minutes and then drain.
2 Combine the tomato sauce, Worcestershire sauce, sugar, paprika, chilli powder and garlic in large non-metallic bowl and mix together well. Add the ribs, cover and marinate in the fridge for at least several hours or overnight if time permits.
3 Cook the ribs on a hot, lightly oiled barbecue grill or flatplate, brushing frequently with the marinade, for 10–15 minutes, or until the ribs are well browned and cooked through. Serve with slices of grilled fresh pineapple.

NUTRITION PER SERVE
Protein 28 g; Fat 10 g; Carbohydrate 21 g;
Dietary Fibre 1 g; Cholesterol 84 mg;
982 kJ (235 cal)

HINT: If time is short, toss the ribs in the marinade and leave at room temperature, covered, for up to 2 hours. The meat will absorb the flavours of the marinade more quickly at room temperature. (This principle applies to all marinades.)

NOTES: Ribs can be bought as a long piece or cut into individual pieces. If chopping ribs yourself, you will need a sharp cleaver. Alternatively, ribs can be cooked in one piece and chopped into pieces after cooking, when the bone is softer. A longer cooking time will be required if the ribs are to be cooked as a single piece.
    Pork ribs can also be used in this recipe. Use either the thick, meaty ribs, which are like beef ribs, or the long thin spare ribs, also known as American-style ribs. Pork spare ribs have less meat so a shorter cooking time is required.

Cook the ribs in a large pan of boiling water for 5 minutes before marinating.

Cook the ribs until they are well browned and cooked through, basting frequently.

FISH BURGERS WITH TARTARE SAUCE

Preparation time: 30 minutes +
   1 hour refrigeration
Total cooking time: 25 minutes
Serves 4

500 g (1 lb) white fish fillets
2 tablespoons finely chopped
   fresh parsley
2 tablespoons finely chopped
   fresh dill
2 tablespoons lemon juice
1 tablespoon capers, finely chopped
2 finely chopped gherkins
350 g (11 oz) potatoo, cooked and
   mashed
plain flour, for dusting
2 teaspoons olive oil
4 hamburger buns
lettuce leaves
2 Roma tomatoes, sliced

TARTARE SAUCE
1/3 cup (90 g/3 oz) low-fat mayonnaise
1/2 finely chopped gherkin
2 teaspoons capers, finely chopped
1/2 teaspoon malt vinegar
2 teaspoons finely chopped
   fresh parsley
2 teaspoons lemon juice

1 Place the fish fillets in a frying pan and just cover with water. Slowly heat the water, making sure it doesn't boil. Cover and cook over low heat until the fish is just cooked. Drain the fish on paper towels, transfer to a large bowl and flake with a fork. Add the parsley, dill, lemon juice, capers, gherkin and mashed potato, season well and mix thoroughly. Divide into 4 portions and shape into patties, handling the mixture carefully as it is quite soft. Dust lightly with flour and refrigerate on a plate for 1 hour.
2 Meanwhile, make the tartare sauce by mixing all the ingredients thoroughly in a bowl.
3 Heat the olive oil in a large non-stick frying pan, carefully add the patties and cook for 5–6 minutes on each side, or until well browned and heated through.
4 Meanwhile, cut the hamburger buns in half and toast under a grill (broiler). Fill the buns with lettuce leaves, tomato slices, the patties and then a spoonful of tartare sauce. Serve with crunchy potato wedges.

NUTRITION PER SERVE
Protein 40 g; Fat 15 g; Carbohydrate 70 g;
Dietary Fibre 7 g; Cholesterol 95 mg;
2375 kJ (565 cal)

Pour in enough water to cover the fish fillets and slowly heat the water.

Mix the flaked fish with the herbs, potato, juice, capers, gherkin and seasoning.

slow-cooked classics

LANCASHIRE HOTPOT

Preparation time: 20 minutes
Total cooking time: 2 hours
Serves 8

8 forequarter chops, cut 2.5 cm
    (1 inch) thick
4 lamb kidneys, cut into quarters,
    cores removed
3 tablespoons plain flour
30 g (1 oz) butter
4 potatoes, thinly sliced
2 large onions, sliced
2 celery sticks, chopped
1 large carrot, peeled and chopped
1³/₄ cups (440 ml/14 fl oz) chicken or
    beef stock
200 g (6¹/₂ oz) button mushrooms,
    sliced
2 teaspoons chopped fresh thyme
1 tablespoon Worcestershire sauce

1 Preheat the oven to warm 160°C
(315°F/Gas 2–3). Lightly brush a large
casserole dish with oil. Trim the meat
of fat and sinew and toss the chops
and kidneys in flour, shaking off the
excess. Heat the butter in a large frying
pan and brown the chops quickly on
both sides. Remove the chops from the
pan and brown the kidneys. Layer half
the potato slices in the base of the dish
and place the chops and kidneys on
top of them.

2 Add the onion, celery and carrot to
the pan and cook until the carrot
begins to brown. Layer on top of the
chops and kidneys. Sprinkle the
remaining flour over the base of the
pan and cook, stirring, until dark
brown. Gradually pour in the stock
and bring to the boil, stirring. Add
the mushrooms, salt, pepper, thyme
and Worcestershire sauce, reduce

the heat and leave to simmer for
10 minutes. Pour into the casserole
dish.

3 Layer the remaining potato over the
top of the casserole, to cover the meat
and vegetables. Cover and cook in the
oven for 1¹/₄ hours. Remove the lid

and cook for a further 30 minutes, or
until the potatoes are brown.

NUTRITION PER SERVE
Protein 40 g; Fat 10 g; Carbohydrate 11 g;
Dietary Fibre 3 g; Cholesterol 170 mg;
1227 kJ (295 cal)

Toss the kidneys in flour and then brown in the
pan you used for browning the chops.

Stir in the mushrooms, seasoning, thyme and
Worcestershire sauce.

Layer the remaining potato over the top of the
casserole, covering the meat and vegetables.

CHICKEN IN RICH MUSHROOM SAUCE

Preparation time: 40 minutes
Total cooking time: 1 hour 10 minutes
Serves 4

1.4 kg (2 lb 13 oz) chicken
1 onion, sliced
2 whole cloves
8–10 peppercorns
1 teaspoon salt
90 g (3 oz) butter
500 g (1 lb) mushrooms, sliced
2 cloves garlic, crushed
2 tablespoons plain flour
1/2 cup (125 ml/4 fl oz) cream
1 tablespoon French mustard
1 cup (125 g/4 oz) grated Cheddar
1/2 cup (50 g/1 3/4 oz) stale
    breadcrumbs
1/4 cup (15 g/1/2 oz) finely chopped
    fresh parsley

1 Preheat the oven to moderate 180°C (350°F/Gas 4). Trim the chicken of excess fat and sinew. Cut the chicken into 10 portions. Place the chicken, onion, cloves, peppercorns and salt into a 2 litre ovenproof dish with 3 cups (750 ml/24 fl oz) water. Bake for 30 minutes. Remove the chicken from the dish and strain the liquid into a bowl, reserving 2 cups (500 ml/16 fl oz). Melt half the butter in a frying pan. Add the mushrooms and cook until soft. Add the garlic and cook for 2 minutes. Transfer the mixture to a bowl.
2 Melt the remaining butter in the pan. Add the flour and cook for 2 minutes. Gradually add the reserved liquid and stir until smooth. Bring to the boil. Remove from the heat and stir in the cream, mustard and mushrooms.

3 Return the chicken and sauce to the dish. Sprinkle with the combined Cheddar, breadcrumbs and parsley. Bake for 30 minutes.

NUTRITION PER SERVE
Protein 75 g; Fat 60 g; Carbohydrate 16 g; Dietary Fibre 4.5 g; Cholesterol 275 mg; 3727 kJ (890 Cal)

Place the chicken, onion, cloves, peppercorns and salt into an ovenproof dish.

Remove the sauce from the heat and stir in the cream, mustard and mushrooms.

Sprinkle the chicken and sauce with the combined cheese, breadcrumbs and parsley.

CURRIED BEEF SAUSAGES

Preparation time: 20 minutes
Total cooking time: 45 minutes
Serves 6–8

1 onion, chopped
2 cloves garlic
1 teaspoon chopped fresh ginger
2 teaspoons curry powder
1 teaspoon chilli powder
1½ teaspoons paprika
3 teaspoons poppy seeds
2 tablespoons oil

1.25 kg (2 lb 8 oz) medium-size good-quality beef sausages
6 tomatoes, skinned, quartered and seeded
2 tablespoons mango chutney
1²/₃ cups (420 ml/13 fl oz) coconut milk

1 Place the onion, garlic, ginger, curry powder, chilli powder, paprika and poppy seeds in a food processor, and process until smooth.
2 Heat 1 tablespoon of the oil in a saucepan and cook for 6–8 minutes, or until browned. Remove and wipe

out the pan with paper towels. Leave the sausages to cool and slice into 1 cm (½ inch) thick pieces.
3 Heat the remaining oil in the pan, add the spice paste and cook, stirring, for 2 minutes, or until fragrant. Mix in the tomato, mango chutney, coconut milk and sausages, and simmer, covered, for 20 minutes, stirring occasionally.

NUTRITION PER SERVE (8)
Protein 22 g; Fat 50 g; Carbohydrate 10 g;
Dietary Fibre 6 g; Cholesterol 90 mg;
2407 kJ (575 Cal)

Place the paste ingredients in a food processor and process until smooth.

Cook the sausages in batches in a large frying pan until browned on all sides.

Wipe out the pan with paper towels to remove any excess oil.

VEAL GOULASH

Preparation time: 25 minutes
Total cooking time: 2 hours
Serves 4

500 g (1 lb) veal, cut into 2.5 cm
   (1 inch) pieces
2 tablespoons plain flour
2 tablespoons olive oil
2 onions, thinly sliced
2 cloves garlic, finely chopped
1 tablespoon sweet Hungarian paprika
1 teaspoon ground cumin
440 g (14 oz) can diced tomatoes
2 carrots, sliced
1/2 red capsicum, chopped
1/2 green capsicum, chopped

1 cup (250 ml/8 fl oz) beef stock
1/2 cup (125 ml/4 fl oz) red wine
1/2 cup (125 g/4 fl oz) sour cream
chopped fresh parsley, to garnish

1 Put the veal and flour in a plastic bag and shake to coat the veal with flour. Shake off any excess. Heat 1 tablespoon oil in a large deep heavy-based pan over medium heat. Brown the meat well in batches, then remove the meat and set aside.

2 Add the remaining oil to the pan. Cook the onion, garlic, paprika and cumin for 5 minutes, stirring frequently. Return the meat and any juices to the pan with the tomato, carrot and capsicum. Cover and cook for 10 minutes.

3 Add the stock and wine and season with salt and pepper. Stir well, then cover and simmer over very low heat for 1 1/2 hours. Stir in half the sour cream, season with more salt and pepper if needed and serve garnished with parsley and the remaining sour cream. Delicious served with buttered boiled small potatoes or noodles.

NUTRITION PER SERVE
Protein 30 g; Fat 25 g; Carbohydrate 15 g; Dietary Fibre 4.5 g; Cholesterol 144 mg; 1790 kJ (430 Cal)

NOTE: If you prefer your sauce to be a little thicker, cook, uncovered, for 5 minutes over high heat before adding the sour cream.

Remove any excess fat then cut the veal into 2.5 cm (1 inch) pieces.

Put the veal and flour in a plastic bag and shake to coat.

Heat the oil in a pan, add the veal and brown well in batches.

CHICKEN CACCIATORE

Preparation time: 45 minutes
Total cooking time: 1 hour 20 minutes
Serves 4

4 tomatoes
1.5 kg (3 lb) chicken pieces
20 g (³/₄ oz) butter
1 tablespoon oil
20 g (³/₄ oz) butter, extra
1 large onion, chopped
2 cloves garlic, chopped
1 small green capsicum, chopped
150 g (5 oz) mushrooms, thickly sliced
1 tablespoon plain flour
1 cup (250 ml/8 fl oz) white wine
1 tablespoon white wine vinegar
2 tablespoons tomato paste
¹/₂ cup (90 g/3 oz) small black olives
¹/₃ cup (20 g/³/₄ oz) chopped fresh
    parsley

1 Score a cross in the base of each tomato. Put the tomatoes in a bowl of boiling water for 30 seconds, then transfer to a bowl of cold water. Drain and peel the skin away from the cross. Halve the tomatoes and remove the seeds with a teaspoon. Chop the flesh. Preheat the oven to moderate 180°C (350°F/Gas 4).
2 Remove excess fat from the chicken pieces and pat dry with paper towels. Heat half the butter and oil in a large flameproof casserole. Cook half the chicken over high heat until browned all over, then set aside. Heat the remaining butter and oil and cook the remaining chicken. Set aside.
3 Heat the extra butter in the casserole and cook the onion and garlic for 2–3 minutes. Add the capsicum and mushrooms, and cook, stirring, for 3 minutes. Stir in the flour and cook for 1 minute. Add the wine,

vinegar, tomato and tomato paste and cook, stirring, for 2 minutes, or until slightly thickened.
4 Return the chicken to the casserole and make sure it is covered by the tomato and onion mixture. Place in the oven and cook, covered, for 1 hour, or until the chicken is tender. Stir in the olives and parsley. Season with salt and cracked black pepper and serve with pasta.

NUTRITION PER SERVE
Protein 55 g; Fat 15 g; Carbohydrate 9.5 g; Dietary Fibre 5 g; Cholesterol 125 mg; 1675 kJ (401 Cal)

NOTE: If you prefer a thicker sauce, remove the cooked chicken from the casserole and reduce the sauce over high heat until slightly thickened. Return all the chicken to the casserole and add the olives and parsley.

Drain the tomatoes, then peel away the skin from the cross.

Cut the tomatoes in half and remove the seeds with a teaspoon.

Cook the chicken in batches over high heat until browned all over.

APRICOT CHICKEN

Preparation time: 10 minutes
Total cooking time: 1 hour
Serves 6

6 chicken thigh cutlets
425 ml (14 fl oz) can apricot nectar
40 g (1¹/₄ oz) packet French onion
    soup mix
425 g (14 oz) can apricot halves in
    natural juice, drained
¹/₄ cup (60 g/2 oz) sour cream

1 Preheat the oven to moderate 180°C (350°F/Gas 4). Remove the skin from the chicken thigh cutlets. Put the chicken in an ovenproof dish. Mix the apricot nectar with the French onion

soup mix until well combined, and pour over the chicken.
2 Bake, covered, for 50 minutes, then add the apricot halves and bake for a further 5 minutes. Stir in the sour cream just before serving. Delicious served with creamy mashed potato or rice to soak up the juices.

Pour in the apricot nectar and stir to combine with the soup mix.

NUTRITION PER SERVE
Protein 23 g; Fat 6 g; Carbohydrate 10 g; Dietary Fibre 0 g; Cholesterol 63 mg; 780 kJ (187 Cal)

NOTE: If you are looking for a healthy alternative, you can use low-fat sour cream in place of the full-fat version.

Add the apricot halves to the chicken and bake for 5 minutes more.

LAMB CHOP CASSEROLE

Preparation time: 15 minutes
Total cooking time: 1 hour 15 minutes
Serves 4

6–8 lamb chump chops (see NOTE)
1 tablespoon oil
1 large onion, finely chopped
1/3 cup (90 g/3 oz) redcurrant jelly
1 teaspoon grated lemon rind
1 tablespoon lemon juice
1 tablespoon barbecue sauce
1 tablespoon tomato sauce
1/2 cup (125 ml/4 fl oz) chicken
    stock

1 Trim any fat from the lamb. Preheat the oven to moderate180°C (350°F/ Gas 4). Heat the oil in a large heavy-based frying pan; add the chops and cook over medium-high heat for 2–3 minutes, turning once, until well browned. Remove from the pan and put in a casserole dish.

2 Add the onion to the frying pan and cook over medium heat, stirring frequently, for 5 minutes or until the onion is softened. Add the jelly, lemon rind and juice, barbecue and tomato sauces and stock. Stir for 2–3 minutes until heated through. Pour over the chops and stir well, cover and place in the oven. Cook for 1 hour, or until the meat is tender, turning 2–3 times. Lift out the chops onto a side plate and leave them to keep warm.

3 Pour the sauce into a pan and boil rapidly for 5 minutes until the sauce has thickened and reduced. Return the chops to the sauce before serving.

NUTRITION PER SERVE
Protein 30 g; Fat 11 g; Carbohydrate 13 g; Dietary Fibre 1 g; Cholesterol 95 mg; 1150 kJ (275 cal)

STORAGE TIME: Keep covered and refrigerated for up to 2 days. Suitable to freeze for up to 1 month.

NOTE: Other lamb chop cuts can be used instead of chump.

Once the chops have been well browned, put them in a casserole dish.

Pour the sauce over the chops in the dish and stir to combine.

Use a pair of tongs to turn the chops a couple of times during cooking.

COQ AU VIN

Preparation time: 20 minutes
Total cooking time: 1 hour
Serves 6

2 fresh thyme sprigs
4 fresh parsley sprigs
2 bay leaves
2 kg (4 lb) chicken pieces
plain flour, seasoned with salt
    and freshly ground pepper
1/4 cup (60 ml/2 fl oz) oil
4 thick bacon rashers, sliced
12 pickling onions
2 cloves garlic, crushed
2 tablespoons brandy
1 1/2 cups (375 ml/12 fl oz) red wine

1 1/2 cups (375 ml/12 fl oz) chicken
    stock
1/4 cup (60 g/2 oz) tomato paste
250 g (8 oz) button mushrooms
fresh herbs, for sprinkling

1 To make the bouquet garni, wrap the thyme, parsley and bay leaves in a small square of muslin and tie well with string, or tie them between two 5 cm (2 inch) lengths of celery.

2 Toss the chicken in flour to coat, shaking off any excess. In a heavy-based pan, heat 2 tablespoons of oil and brown the chicken in batches over medium heat. Drain on paper towels.

3 Wipe the pan clean with paper towels and heat the remaining oil. Add the bacon, onions and garlic and cook, stirring, until the onions are browned. Add the chicken, brandy, wine, stock, bouquet garni and tomato paste. Bring to the boil, reduce the heat and simmer, covered, for 30 minutes.

4 Stir in the mushrooms and simmer, uncovered, for 10 minutes, or until the chicken is tender and the sauce has thickened. Remove the bouquet garni, sprinkle with fresh herbs and serve with crusty French bread.

NUTRITION PER SERVE
Protein 80 g; Fat 20 g; Carbohydrate 7 g;
Dietary Fibre 2 g; Cholesterol 180 mg;
2420 kJ (580 Cal)

Wrap the thyme, parsley and bay leaves in a small square of muslin.

In batches, brown the chicken in the hot oil over medium heat.

Return the chicken to the pan with the liquids, bouquet garni and tomato paste.

SILVERSIDE AND PARSLEY SAUCE

Preparation time: 20 minutes + soaking
Total cooking time: 2 hours
Serves 6

1.5 kg (3 lb) corned silverside
1 teaspoon black peppercorns
5 whole cloves
2 bay leaves, torn
2 tablespoons soft brown sugar

PARSLEY SAUCE
30 g (1 oz) butter
1½ tablespoons plain flour
400 ml (13 fl oz) skim milk
½ cup (125 ml/4 fl oz) beef stock
2 tablespoons chopped fresh parsley

1 Soak the corned beef in cold water for 45 minutes, changing the water 3–4 times to reduce the saltiness.
2 Put the beef in a large heavy-based pan with the peppercorns, cloves, bay leaves, brown sugar and enough cold water to just cover. Bring to the boil, then reduce the heat to very low and simmer for 1½–1¾ hours. Turn the meat every 30 minutes and add more water when needed. Do not let the water boil or the beef will be tough. Remove from the pan, wrap in foil and leave to stand for at least 15 minutes before carving. (Save the liquid and use for cooking vegetables.)
3 To make the parsley sauce, melt the butter in a pan over medium heat, and stir in the flour. Cook, stirring with a wooden spoon, for 1 minute. Remove the pan from the heat and pour in the milk and stock, whisking until smooth. Return the pan to the heat and cook, whisking constantly, until the sauce boils and thickens. Reduce the heat and simmer for 2 minutes more. Stir in the parsley and season to taste.
4 Slice the meat across the grain and serve with the sauce.

NUTRITION PER SERVE
Protein 50 g; Fat 15 g; Carbohydrate 10 g; Dietary Fibre 0 g; Cholesterol 100 mg; 1625 kJ (390 cal)

Soak the corned beef in cold water to help eliminate some of the saltiness.

Put the beef, peppercorns, cloves, bay leaves and sugar in a pan and cover with water.

Make sure you turn the meat every half hour or so and don't boil the water or the meat will toughen.

CHICKEN PAPRIKA

Preparation time: 25 minutes
Total cooking time: 45 minutes
Serves 4–6

800 g (1 lb 10 oz) chicken thigh fillets
1/2 cup (60 g/2 oz) plain flour
2 tablespoons oil
2 onions, chopped
1–2 cloves garlic, crushed
2 tablespoons sweet paprika
1/2 cup (125 ml/4 fl oz) good-quality
  red wine
1 tablespoon tomato paste
425 g (14 oz) can tomatoes
200 g (6¹/2 oz) button mushrooms

1/2 cup (125 ml/4 fl oz) chicken stock
2/3 cup (80 g/2³/4 oz) sour cream

1 Rinse the chicken and dry well. Trim the chicken of excess fat and sinew. Cut the chicken into 3 cm (1¹/4 inch) pieces. Season the flour with salt and pepper. Toss the chicken pieces lightly in the seasoned flour, shake off the excess and reserve the flour. Heat half the oil in a large heavy-based pan. Cook the chicken pieces quickly in small batches over medium-high heat. Remove from the pan and drain on paper towels.

2 Heat the remaining oil in the pan and add the onion and garlic. Cook, stirring, until the onion is soft. Add the paprika and reserved flour, and stir for 1 minute. Add the chicken, wine, tomato paste and undrained crushed tomatoes. Bring to the boil, then reduce the heat and simmer, covered, for 15 minutes.

3 Add the mushrooms and chicken stock. Simmer, covered, for a further 10 minutes. Add the sour cream and stir until heated through, but do not allow to boil.

NUTRITION PER SERVE
Protein 35 g; Fat 20 g; Carbohydrate 14 g; Dietary Fibre 3 g; Cholesterol 105 mg; 1668 kJ (399 cal)

Trim the chicken thigh fillets of excess fat and sinew, and cut into pieces.

Add the chicken, red wine, tomato paste and undrained crushed tomatoes.

Stir in the sour cream until heated through, but do not allow to boil.

VEGETABLE CURRY

Preparation time: 20 minutes
Total cooking time: 30 minutes
Serves 6

250 g (8 oz) potatoes, diced
250 g (8 oz) pumpkin, diced
200 g (6¹/₂ oz) cauliflower, broken into
  florets
150 g (5 oz) yellow squash, cut into
  quarters
1 tablespoon oil
2 onions, chopped
3 tablespoons curry powder
400 g (13 oz) can crushed tomatoes

1 cup (250 ml/8 fl oz) vegetable stock
150 g (5 oz) green beans, cut into
  short lengths
¹/₃ cup (90 g/3 oz) natural yoghurt
¹/₄ cup (30 g/1 oz) sultanas

1 Bring a saucepan of water to the boil, add the potato and pumpkin, and cook for 6 minutes, then remove. Add the cauliflower and squash, cook for 4 minutes, then remove.
2 Heat the oil in a large saucepan, add the onion and cook, stirring, over medium heat for 8 minutes, or until starting to brown.
3 Add the curry powder and stir for 1 minute, or until fragrant. Stir in the crushed tomato and vegetable stock.
4 Add the parboiled potato, pumpkin, cauliflower and squash and cook for 5 minutes, then add the green beans and cook for a further 2–3 minutes, or until the vegetables are just tender.
5 Add the yoghurt and sultanas, and stir to combine. Simmer for 3 minutes, or until thickened slightly. Season to taste and serve with lemon wedges.

NUTRITION PER SERVE
Protein 7 g; Fat 8.5 g; Carbohydrate 20 g;
Dietary Fibre 7 g; Cholesterol 2.5 mg;
805 kJ (192 cal)

Cook the onion over medium heat until it is starting to brown.

Add the beans and cook until the vegetables are just tender.

Add the yoghurt and sultanas and simmer until thickened slightly.

CHICKEN MOLE

Preparation time: 25 minutes
Total cooking time: 1 hour
Serves 4

8 chicken drumsticks
plain flour, for dusting
cooking oil spray
1 large onion, finely chopped
2 cloves garlic, finely chopped
1 teaspoon ground cumin
1 teaspoon chilli powder
2 teaspoons cocoa powder
440 g (14 oz) can tomatoes, roughly
    chopped
440 ml (14 fl oz) tomato purée

1 cup (250 ml/8 fl oz) chicken stock
toasted almonds, to garnish
chopped fresh parsley, to garnish

1 Remove and discard the chicken skin. Wipe the chicken with paper towels and lightly dust with flour. Spray a large, deep, non-stick frying pan with oil. Cook the chicken for 8 minutes over high heat, turning until golden brown. Remove and set aside.
2 Add the onion, garlic, cumin, chilli powder, cocoa, 1 teaspoon salt, $1/2$ teaspoon black pepper and $1/4$ cup (60 ml/2 fl oz) water to the pan and cook for 5 minutes, or until softened.
3 Stir in the tomato, tomato purée and chicken stock. Bring to the boil, then add the chicken drumsticks, cover and simmer for 45 minutes, or until tender. Uncover and simmer for 5 minutes, until the mixture is thick. Garnish with the almonds and parsley. Delicious with kidney beans.

NUTRITION PER SERVE
Protein 25 g; Fat 7 g; Carbohydrate 10 g;
Dietary Fibre 4 g; Cholesterol 100 mg;
910 kJ (220 Cal)

NOTE: This is a traditional Mexican dish, usually flavoured with a special type of dark chocolate rather than cocoa powder.

Pull the skin off the chicken drumsticks, then wipe the chicken with paper towels.

Turn the chicken until brown on all sides, then remove from the pan.

Stir in the onion, garlic, cumin, chilli powder, cocoa, salt, pepper and water.

BEEF CARBONNADE

Preparation time: 15 minutes
Total cooking time: 3 hours 25 minutes
Serves 4

1 leek, green part only
1 bay leaf
1 sprig fresh thyme
1 sprig celery leaves
4 sprigs fresh parsley
2 tablespoons butter
1 tablespoon oil
1 kg (2 lb) chuck or stewing steak,
    cubed
2 onions, sliced
2 cloves garlic, crushed
2 tablespoons plain flour
1½ cups (375 ml/12 fl oz) brown ale
    or stout
1 long bread stick
2 teaspoons French mustard
2 teaspoons butter, softened

1 To make a bouquet garni, wrap the green part of the leek around the bay leaf, thyme sprig, celery leaves and parsley, then tie with string. Leave a long tail to the string for easy removal.

2 Preheat the oven to moderate 180°C (350°F/Gas 4). Heat the butter and oil in a large pan and cook the beef in batches for 3–4 minutes, or until well browned. Remove from the pan. Lower the heat and cook the onion and garlic for 4 minutes, or until translucent. Sprinkle in the flour, stir well, then cook for 1 minute. Combine the beer with 1½ cups (375 ml/12 fl oz) water and add the pan. Stir well, scraping the pan to incorporate ingredients that are stuck to the base. Bring to the boil and return the meat to the pan. Add the bouquet garni and return to the boil. Transfer to a 2.5 litre casserole dish, cover well with foil and cook gently in the oven for 2½ hours.

3 Cut the bread into 2 cm (3/4 inch) slices and spread with the combined mustard and butter. Remove the casserole from the oven, take out the bouquet garni and skim off any fat. Put the bread slices on the surface of the casserole, mustard-side-up, and press down gently to cover with juice. Return to the oven and cook, uncovered, for another 30–40 minutes, or until the bread becomes crusty. Serve with steamed green vegetables.

NUTRITION PER SERVE
Protein 60 g; Fat 25 g; Carbohydrate 30 g;
Dietary Fibre 3.5 g; Cholesterol 195 mg;
2455 kJ (585 Cal)

Leave a long tail of string on the bouquet garni for easy removal.

Cook the beef in batches until well browned all over.

MOROCCAN CHICKEN

Preparation time: 20 minutes +
 2 hours marinating
Total cooking time: 1 hour 25 minutes
Serves 4

8 large chicken drumsticks
3 cloves garlic, crushed
1 teaspoon grated fresh ginger
1 teaspoon ground turmeric
2 teaspoons ground cumin
1 teaspoon ground cardamom
1 teaspoon finely grated lemon rind
2 tablespoons oil
1 onion, sliced
2 cups (500 ml/16 fl oz) chicken stock

6 pitted dates, chopped
1/3 cup (20 g/3/4 oz) shredded coconut

1 Trim the chicken of excess fat and sinew. Place the chicken in a large bowl. Combine the garlic, ginger, turmeric, cumin, cardamom and rind in a small bowl. Add to the chicken and stir to completely coat. Cover and marinate for 2 hours.
2 Preheat the oven to moderate 180°C (350°F/Gas 4). Heat the oil in a large heavy-based frying pan. Cook the chicken quickly over medium heat until well browned. Drain on paper towels. Place the chicken in an ovenproof casserole dish.
3 Add the onion to the pan and cook, stirring, for 5 minutes, or until soft. Add the cooked onion, chicken stock, dates and shredded coconut to the casserole dish. Cover and bake for 1 hour 15 minutes, or until the chicken is tender, stirring occasionally.

NUTRITION PER SERVE
Protein 47 g; Fat 18 g; Carbohydrate 9 g; Dietary Fibre 2.8 g; Cholesterol 100 mg; 1622 kJ (388 Cal)

NOTE: The chicken may be left to marinate overnight in the refrigerator.

VARIATION: Dried apricots or prunes are great alteratives to dates.

Add the combined garlic, ginger, turmeric, cumin, cardamom and lemon rind to the chicken.

Drain the chicken on paper towels, then place in an ovenproof casserole dish.

Add the onion, stock, dates and coconut to the casserole dish.

CHILLI CON CARNE

Preparation time: 25 minutes +
  overnight soaking
Total cooking time: 2 hours 15 minutes
Serves 6

185 g (6 oz) dried black eye beans
650 g (1 lb 5 oz) tomatoes
1½ tablespoons oil
900 g (1 lb 13 oz) trimmed chuck
  steak, cut into chunks
3 onions, thinly sliced
2 cloves garlic, chopped
2 teaspoons ground cumin
1 tablespoon paprika
½ teaspoon ground allspice
1–2 teaspoons chilli powder
1 tablespoon soft brown sugar
1 tablespoon red wine vinegar

1 Put the beans in a bowl, cover with plenty of water and leave overnight to soak. Drain well. Score a cross in the base of each tomato. Put the tomatoes in a bowl of boiling water for 30 seconds, then transfer to a bowl of cold water. Drain and peel the skin away from the cross. Halve the tomatoes and remove the seeds with a teaspoon. Chop the flesh finely.

2 Heat 1 tablespoon of the oil in a large heavy-based pan and add half the meat. Cook over medium-high heat for 2 minutes, or until well browned. Remove from the pan and repeat with the remaining meat, then remove from the pan.

3 Add the rest of the oil to the pan and add the onion. Cook over medium heat for 5 minutes, or until softened. Add the garlic and spices and cook, stirring, for 1 minute, or until aromatic. Add 2 cups (500 ml/16 fl oz) water and stir. Return the meat to the pan with the beans and tomatoes. Bring to the boil, then reduce the heat to low and simmer, partially covered, for 2 hours, or until the meat is tender and the chilli con carne is thick and dryish, stirring occasionally. Towards the end of the cooking time the mixture may start to catch, so add a little water if necessary. Stir through the sugar and vinegar, and season with salt to taste. Serve with flour tortillas, grated low-fat cheese and lime wedges.

NUTRITION PER SERVE
Protein 43 g; Fat 10 g; Carbohydrate 54 g;
Dietary Fibre 10 g; Cholesterol 100 mg;
2040 kJ (486 cal)

Soak the black eye beans in a bowl of water overnight before cooking them.

Drain the tomatoes then carefully peel the skin away from the cross.

Remove the tomato seeds with a teaspoon and then finely chop the flesh.

PORK AND APPLE BRAISE

Preparation time: 20 minutes
Total cooking time: 40 minutes
Serves 4

1 tablespoon oil
1 large onion, thinly sliced
1 clove garlic, chopped
2 teaspoons soft brown sugar
2 green apples, cut into wedges
4 pork loin steaks or medallions
2 tablespoons brandy
2 tablespoons seeded mustard

1 cup (250 ml/8 fl oz) chicken stock
1/2 cup (140 g/5 oz) pitted prunes
1/2 cup (125 ml/4 fl oz) light cream

1 Heat the oil in a large heavy-based pan. Cook the onion and garlic for 10 minutes over low heat, stirring often, until softened and golden brown. Add the sugar and apple and cook, stirring regularly, until the apple begins to brown. Remove the apple and onion from the pan.
2 Reheat the pan and lightly brown the pork steaks, two at a time, then return them all to the pan. Add the brandy and stir until it has nearly all

evaporated. Add the mustard and stock. Simmer over low heat, covered, for 15 minutes.
3 Return the apple to the pan with the prunes and cream and simmer for 10 minutes, or until the pork is tender. Season to taste before serving.

NUTRITION PER SERVE
Protein 25 g; Fat 12 g; Carbohydrate 22 g;
Dietary Fibre 4 g; Cholesterol 55 mg;
1250 kJ (298 cal)

HINT: Take care not to overcook pork or it can become tough and dry.

Stir the apple regularly over the heat until it begins to brown.

Brown the pork steaks two at a time and then return them all to the pan.

Put the browned apple back in the pan with the prunes and cream.

CHICKEN AND MUSHROOM CASSEROLE

Preparation time: 20 minutes
Total cooking time: 1 hour
Serves 4

20 g (³/₄ oz) dried porcini mushrooms
¹/₄ cup (30 g/1 oz) plain flour
1.5 kg (3 lb) chicken pieces
2 tablespoons oil
1 large onion, chopped
2 cloves garlic, crushed
¹/₄ cup (60 ml/2 fl oz) chicken stock
¹/₃ cup (80 ml/2³/₄ fl oz) white wine
425 g (14 oz) can peeled whole
    tomatoes
1 tablespoon balsamic vinegar
3 fresh thyme sprigs
1 bay leaf
300 g (10 oz) field mushrooms, thickly
    sliced

1 Preheat the oven to moderate 180°C (350°F/Gas 4). Put the porcini mushrooms in a bowl and cover with ¹/₄ cup (60 ml/2 fl oz) boiling water. Leave for 5 minutes, or until the mushrooms are rehydrated.
2 Season the flour with salt and pepper. Lightly toss the chicken in flour to coat and shake off any excess.
3 Heat the oil in a flameproof casserole and cook the chicken in batches until well browned all over. Set aside. Add the onion and garlic to the casserole and cook for 3–5 minutes, or until the onion softens. Stir in the stock.
4 Return the chicken to the casserole with the porcini mushrooms and any remaining liquid, wine, tomatoes, vinegar, thyme and bay leaf. Cover and cook in the oven for 30 minutes.
5 After 30 minutes, remove the lid and add the field mushrooms. Return to the oven and cook, uncovered, for 15–20 minutes, or until the sauce thickens slightly. Serve immediately.

NUTRITION PER SERVE
Protein 55 g; Fat 10 g; Carbohydrate 7 g;
Dietary Fibre 4 g; Cholesterol 115 mg;
1515 kJ (360 cal)

Cover the porcini mushrooms with boiling water and soak until rehydrated.

Lightly toss the chicken pieces in the flour and shake off any excess.

Add the chicken to the casserole and cook in batches until browned.

ROGAN JOSH

Preparation time: 25 minutes
Total cooking time: 1 hour 40 minutes
Serves 6

1 kg (2 lb) boned leg of lamb
1 tablespoon oil
2 onions, chopped
1/2 cup (125 g/4 oz) low-fat natural
    yoghurt
1 teaspoon chilli powder
1 tablespoon ground coriander
2 teaspoons ground cumin
1 teaspoon ground cardamom
1/2 teaspoon ground cloves
1 teaspoon ground turmeric
3 cloves garlic, crushed

1 tablespoon grated fresh ginger
400 g (13 oz) can chopped tomatoes
1/4 cup (30 g/1 oz) slivered almonds
1 teaspoon garam masala
chopped fresh coriander leaves,
    for serving

1 Trim the lamb of any fat or sinew and cut into small cubes.
2 Heat the oil in a large saucepan, add the onion and cook, stirring, for 5 minutes, or until soft. Stir in the yoghurt, chilli powder, coriander, cumin, cardamom, cloves, turmeric, garlic and ginger. Add the tomato and 1 teaspoon salt and simmer for 5 minutes.
3 Add the lamb and stir until coated. Cover and cook over low heat, stirring

occasionally, for 1–1 1/2 hours, or until the lamb is tender. Uncover and simmer until the liquid thickens.
4 Meanwhile, toast the almonds in a dry frying pan over medium heat for 3–4 minutes, shaking the pan gently, until the nuts are golden brown. Remove from the pan at once to prevent them burning.
5 Add the garam masala to the curry and mix through well. Sprinkle the slivered almonds and coriander leaves over the top and serve.

NUTRITION PER SERVE
Protein 40 g; Fat 13 g; Carbohydrate 5.5 g;
Dietary Fibre 2 g; Cholesterol 122 mg;
1236 kJ (295 Cal)

Cook the onion in the oil for 5 minutes, or until it is soft.

Remove the lid from the pan and simmer until the liquid thickens.

Toast the almonds in a dry frying pan until they are golden brown.

COUNTRY BEEF STEW

Preparation time: 40 minutes
Total cooking time: 2 hours 10 minutes
Serves 8

1 small eggplant, cubed
2–3 tablespoons olive oil
2 red onions, sliced
2 cloves garlic, crushed
1 kg (2 lb) chuck steak, cubed
1 teaspoon ground coriander
1/2 teaspoon allspice
3/4 teaspoon sweet paprika
6 ripe tomatoes, chopped
1 cup (250 ml/8 fl oz) red wine
3 cups (750 ml/24 fl oz) beef stock
2 tablespoons tomato paste
250 g (8 oz) baby new potatoes, halved
2 celery sticks, sliced
3 carrots, chopped
2 bay leaves
3 tablespoons chopped fresh parsley

1 Put the eggplant in a colander, sprinkle generously with salt and leave for 20 minutes. Rinse, pat dry with paper towels and set aside.
2 Heat the oil in a large heavy-based pan and cook the onion for 5 minutes until soft; add the garlic and cook for 1 minute. Remove and set aside. Add the eggplant and brown for 5 minutes. Remove and set aside. Brown the meat in batches over medium heat, sprinkle with the spices, season and cook for 1–2 minutes. Add the tomato, onion, wine, stock and tomato paste and bring to the boil. Reduce the heat and simmer, covered, for 25 minutes.
3 Add the potato, celery, carrot and bay leaves, bring to the boil, reduce the heat, cover and simmer for 1 hour. Add the eggplant and simmer for 30 minutes, uncovered. Lift out the bay leaves and stir in the parsley.

NUTRITION PER SERVE
Protein 30 g; Fat 10 g; Carbohydrate 10 g;
Dietary Fibre 4 g; Cholesterol 85 mg;
1160 kJ (280 cal)

Put the eggplant in a colander and sprinkle with salt to draw out any bitterness.

Add the tomato, onion, wine, stock and tomato paste to the pan.

Add the potato, celery, carrot and bay leaves to the pan.

CHICKEN PROVENCALE

Preparation time: 15 minutes
Total cooking time: 1 hour 20 minutes
Serves 6

1 tablespoon olive oil
1.5 kg (3 lb) chicken pieces
1 onion, chopped
1 red capsicum, chopped
1/3 cup (80 ml/2³/₄ fl oz) white wine
1/3 cup (80 ml/2³/₄ fl oz) chicken stock
425 g (14 oz) can chopped tomatoes
2 tablespoons tomato paste
1/2 cup (90 g/3 oz) black olives
4 tablespoons shredded fresh basil

1 Heat the oil in a saucepan over high heat, add the chicken, in batches, and cook for 3–4 minutes, or until browned. Return all the chicken to the pan and add the onion and capsicum. Cook for 2–3 minutes, or until the onion is soft.

2 Add the wine, stock, tomatoes, tomato paste and olives and bring to the boil. Reduce the heat, cover and simmer for 30 minutes. Remove the lid, turn the chicken pieces over and cook for another 30 minutes, or until the chicken is tender and the sauce thickened. Season to taste, sprinkle with the basil and serve with rice.

NUTRITION PER SERVE
Protein 35 g; Fat 10 g; Carbohydrate 5 g; Dietary Fibre 2 g; Cholesterol 115 mg;
1133 kJ (270 cal)

Once the chicken is browned, return it all to the pan with the onion and capsicum.

Just before serving, season and sprinkle with the shredded basil.

PRAWN CURRY

Preparation time: 25 minutes
Total cooking time: 15 minutes
Serves 6

1 tablespoon butter
1 onion, finely chopped
1 clove garlic, crushed
1½ tablespoons curry powder
2 tablespoons plain flour
2 cups (500 ml/16 fl oz) skim milk

1 kg (2 lb) raw prawns, peeled and deveined
1½ tablespoons lemon juice
2 teaspoons sherry
1 tablespoon finely chopped fresh parsley

1 Heat the butter in a large saucepan. Add the onion and garlic, and cook for 5 minutes, or until softened. Add the curry powder and cook for 1 minute, then stir in the flour and cook for a further 1 minute.

2 Remove from the heat and stir in the milk until smooth. Return to the heat and stir constantly until the sauce has thickened. Simmer for 2 minutes and then stir in the prawns. Continue to simmer for 5 minutes, or until the prawns are just cooked.

3 Stir in the lemon juice, sherry and parsley and serve immediately with rice.

NUTRITION PER SERVE
Protein 38 g; Fat 12 g; Carbohydrate 9 g;
Dietary Fibre 1.5 g; Cholesterol 280 mg;
1247 kJ (298 Cal)

Add the garlic and onion to the butter and cook until softened.

Return the saucepan to the heat and stir the curry constantly until thickened.

Add the prawns and continue to simmer until they are just cooked.

BEEF POT ROAST

Preparation time: 15 minutes
Total cooking time: 3 hours 15 minutes
Serves 6

300 g (10 oz) small pickling onions
2 carrots
3 parsnips, peeled
30 g (1 oz) butter
1–1.5 kg (2–3 lb) piece of silverside,
    trimmed of fat (see NOTE)
1/4 cup (60 ml/2 fl oz) dry red wine
1 large tomato, finely chopped
1 cup (250 ml/8 fl oz) beef stock

1 Put the onions in a heatproof bowl and cover with boiling water. Leave for 1 minute, then drain well. Allow to cool and then peel off the skins.

2 Cut the carrots and parsnips in half lengthways then into even-sized pieces. Heat half the butter in a large heavy-based pan that will tightly fit the meat (it will shrink during cooking), add the onions, carrot and parsnip and cook, stirring, over medium-high heat until browned. Remove from the pan.
3 Add the remaining butter to the pan and add the meat, browning well all over. Increase the heat to high and pour in the wine. Bring to the boil, then add the tomato and stock. Return to the boil, then reduce the heat to low, cover and simmer for 2 hours, turning once. Add the vegetables and simmer, covered, for 1 hour.
4 Remove the meat from the pan and put it on a board ready for carving. Cover with foil and leave it to stand while you finish the sauce.

5 Increase the heat to high and boil the pan juices with the vegetables for 10 minutes to reduce and thicken slightly. Skim off any fat and taste before seasoning. Serve the meat and vegetables with the pan juices. Serve with mustard.

NUTRITION PER SERVE
Protein 60 g; Fat 10 g; Carbohydrate 95 g; Dietary Fibre 3.5 g; Cholesterol 185 mg; 1690 kJ (405 cal)

NOTE: Eye of silverside is a tender, long shaped cut of silverside which carves easily into serving-sized pieces. A regular piece of silverside or topside may be substituted.

Put the pickling onions in a bowl and cover with boiling water.

Add the piece of meat to the pan and brown well on all sides.

Put the vegetables in with the meat, then cover and simmer for 1 hour.

CHILLI CON POLLO

Preparation time: 10 minutes
Total cooking time: 45 minutes
Serves 4

1 tablespoon olive oil
1 onion, finely chopped
500 g (1 lb) chicken mince
1–2 teaspoons mild chilli powder
440 g (14 oz) can chopped tomatoes
2 tablespoons tomato paste
1–2 teaspoons soft brown sugar
425 g (13 oz) can red kidney beans,
    rinsed and drained

1 Heat the oil in a large saucepan. Add the onion and cook over medium heat for 3 minutes, or until soft. Increase the heat and add the chicken. Cook until browned, breaking up any lumps with a wooden spoon.
2 Add the chilli powder and cook for 1 minute. Add the tomato, tomato paste and $1/2$ cup (125 ml/4 fl oz) water and stir well.
3 Bring to the boil, then reduce the heat and simmer for 30 minutes. Stir through the sugar to taste and the kidney beans and heat through. Season and serve with baked corn chips and low-fat natural yoghurt.

NUTRITION PER SERVE
Protein 37 g; Fat 8.5 g; Carbohydrate 20 g;
Dietary Fibre 9 g; Cholesterol 60 mg;
1305 kJ (312 cal)

Cook the mince until it has browned, breaking up any lumps with a wooden spoon.

Add the tomato, tomato paste and water and stir well to combine.

Simmer for 30 minutes, then stir in the kidney beans and heat through.

LAMB CASSEROLE WITH BEANS

Preparation time: 25 minutes + overnight soaking
Total cooking time: 2 hours 15 minutes
Serves 6

1½ cups (300 g/10 oz) borlotti or red kidney beans
1 kg (2 lb) boned leg lamb
1 tablespoon olive oil
2 rashers bacon, rind removed, chopped
1 large onion, chopped
2 cloves garlic, crushed
1 large carrot, chopped
2 cups (500 ml/16 fl oz) dry red wine
1 tablespoon tomato paste
1½ cups (375 ml/12 fl oz) beef stock
2 large sprigs fresh rosemary
2 sprigs fresh thyme

1 Put the beans in a bowl and cover with plenty of water. Leave to soak overnight, then drain well.
2 Preheat the oven to warm 160°C (315°F/Gas 2–3). Trim any fat from the lamb and cut into bite-sized cubes.
3 Heat the oil in a large flameproof casserole and brown the lamb in two batches over high heat for 2 minutes. Remove all the lamb from the casserole and set aside.
4 Add the bacon and onion to the casserole. Cook over medium heat for 3 minutes, or until the onion is soft. Add the garlic and carrot and cook for 1 minute, or until aromatic.

5 Return the lamb and any juices to the pan, increase the heat to high and add the wine. Bring to the boil and cook for 2 minutes. Add the beans, tomato paste, stock, rosemary and thyme, bring to the boil, then cover and cook in the oven for 2 hours, or until the meat is tender. Stir occasionally during cooking. Skim off any fat from the surface and then season and remove the herb sprigs before serving.

NUTRITION PER SERVE
Protein 50 g; Fat 10 g; Carbohydrate 48 g; Dietary Fibre 9 g; Cholesterol 117 mg; 2367 kJ (565 cal)

Remove the fat from the lamb then cut it into bite-sized cubes.

Heat the oil in the casserole and brown the lamb in two batches.

Return the meat and juices to the pan, add the wine, and bring to the boil.

BEEF STROGANOFF

Preparation time: 20 minutes
Total cooking time: 25 minutes
Serves 4

500 g (1 lb) rump steak
cooking oil spray
1 onion, sliced
1/4 teaspoon paprika
250 g (8 oz) button mushrooms, halved
2 tablespoons tomato paste
1/2 cup (125 ml/4 fl oz) beef stock
1/2 cup (125 ml/4 fl oz) low-fat evaporated milk
3 teaspoons cornflour
3 tablespoons chopped fresh parsley

1 Remove any excess fat from the steak and slice into thin strips. Cook in batches in a large, lightly greased non-stick frying pan over high heat, until just cooked. Remove from the pan.
2 Lightly spray the pan and cook the onion, paprika and mushrooms over medium heat until the onion has softened. Add the meat, tomato paste, stock and 1/2 cup (125 ml/4 fl oz) water. Bring to the boil, then reduce the heat and simmer for 10 minutes.
3 In a small bowl, mix the evaporated milk with the cornflour. Add to the pan and stir until the sauce boils and thickens. Sprinkle with parsley.

NUTRITION PER SERVE
Protein 35 g; Fat 4 g; Carbohydrate 8 g;
Dietary Fibre 2.5 g; Cholesterol 85 mg;
900 kJ (215 Cal)

Slice the rump steak into thin strips after removing any excess fat.

Stir the onion, paprika and mushrooms until the onion has softened.

Stir the evaporated milk into the cornflour until the mixture is smooth.

CHICKEN CHASSEUR

Preparation time: 20 minutes
Total cooking time: 1 hour 30 minutes
Serves 4

1 kg (2 lb) chicken thigh fillets
1 tablespoon oil
1 clove garlic, crushed
1 large onion, sliced
100 g (3¹/₂ oz) button mushrooms, sliced
1 teaspoon thyme leaves
400 g (13 oz) can chopped tomatoes
¹/₄ cup (60 ml/2 fl oz) chicken stock
¹/₄ cup (60 ml/2 fl oz) white wine
1 tablespoon tomato paste

1 Preheat the oven to moderate 180°C (350°F/Gas 4). Trim the chicken of any fat and sinew. Heat the oil in a heavy-based frying pan and brown the chicken in batches over medium heat. Drain on paper towels and then transfer to a casserole dish.
2 Add the garlic, onion and mushrooms to the pan and cook over medium heat for 5 minutes, or until soft. Add to the chicken with the thyme and tomatoes.
3 Combine the stock, wine and tomato paste and pour over the chicken. Cover and bake for 1¹/₄ hours, or until the chicken is tender and cooked through.

NUTRITION PER SERVE
Protein 60 g; Fat 12 g; Carbohydrate 6 g; Dietary Fibre 2 g; Cholesterol 125 mg; 1710 kJ (410 cal)

STORAGE TIME: Best cooked a day in advance to let the flavours develop.

Brown the chicken in the hot oil over medium heat and drain on paper towels.

Add the garlic, onion and mushrooms to the pan and cook until soft.

Pour the combined stock, wine and tomato paste over the chicken mixture.

TAGINE OF LAMB WITH QUINCE AND LEMON

Preparation time: 25 minutes
Total cooking time: 2 hours 10 minutes
Serves 4

1.5 kg (3 lb) boned shoulder of lamb,
    cut into 12 even pieces
1 onion, finely chopped
2 cloves garlic, crushed
1 cinnamon stick
1 teaspoon ground ginger
1/2 teaspoon saffron threads
1 large quince, peeled, seeded and cut
    into 12 pieces
1/4 cup (90 ml/3 fl oz) honey

1 teaspoon ground cinnamon
1/2 preserved lemon

1 Trim the lamb of excess fat and place in a large pan. Add the onion, garlic, cinnamon stick, ginger and saffron and enough cold water to cover. Slowly bring to the boil, stirring occasionally. Reduce the heat, cover and simmer for 45 minutes. Transfer the meat to a casserole dish.
2 Add the quince, honey and ground cinnamon to the cooking liquid and simmer for 15 minutes, or until the quince is tender. Discard the cinnamon, remove the quince and add to the meat, reserving the liquid.

3 Preheat the oven to moderate 180°C (350°F/Gas 4). Boil the cooking liquid for 30 minutes, or until reduced by half, then pour over the meat and quince. Remove and discard the flesh from the lemon. Slice the rind thinly, then add to the meat. Cover and bake for 40 minutes, or until the meat is tender.

NUTRITION PER SERVE
Protein 80 g; Fat 15 g; Carbohydrate 20 g;
Dietary Fibre 3 g; Cholesterol 250 mg;
2160 kJ (515 cal)

HINT: As you work, place the peeled quince in water with a little lemon juice to prevent discolouring.

Add the onion, garlic, cinnamon stick, ginger, saffron and cold water to the lamb.

Add the quince, honey and ground cinnamon to the cooking liquid.

Remove and discard the flesh from the preserved lemon and slice the rind thinly.

BOSTON BAKED BEANS

Preparation time: 25 minutes +
  6 hours soaking
Total cooking time: 1 hour 35 minutes
Serves 6

1³/4 cups (350 g/11 oz) dried
   cannellini beans (see NOTE)
1 whole ham hock
2 onions, chopped
2 tablespoons tomato paste
1 tablespoon Worcestershire sauce
1 tablespoon molasses
1 teaspoon French mustard
¹/4 cup (45 g/1¹/2 oz) brown sugar
¹/2 cup (125 ml/4 fl oz) tomato juice

1 Cover the beans with cold water and soak for at least 6 hours or overnight (see NOTE).
2 Drain the beans, rinse them well and place in a large pan. Add the ham hock and cover with cold water. Bring to the boil, then reduce the heat and simmer, covered, for 25 minutes, or until the beans are tender. Preheat the oven to warm 160°C (315°F/Gas 2–3).
3 Remove the ham hock from the pan and set aside to cool. Drain the beans, reserving 1 cup (250 ml/8 fl oz) of the cooking liquid. Trim the ham of all skin, fat and sinew, then roughly chop the meat and discard the bone.
4 Transfer the meat and beans to a 2 litre casserole dish. Add the reserved liquid and all remaining ingredients. Mix gently, then cover and bake for 1 hour. Serve with toast.

NUTRITION PER SERVE
Protein 28 g; Fat 5 g; Carbohydrate 30 g;
Dietary Fibre 2 g; Cholesterol 60 mg;
1090 kJ (260 cal)

NOTE: Any type of dried bean can be used in this recipe.

If you don't have 6 hours to soak the beans, to quick-soak beans, place them in a pan, add hot water to cover, bring slowly to the boil, then remove from the heat. Leave to soak for 1 hour before draining and using.

Cooked beans can be frozen in small quantities.

Place the drained beans in a large pan. Add the ham hock and cover with cold water.

Trim the ham of all fat, skin and sinew, then roughly chop the meat.

Add the reserved liquid and remaining ingredients to the meat and beans.

BUTTER CHICKEN

Preparation time: 30 minutes
+ 4 hours marinating
Total cooking time: 20 minutes
Serves 4

1 kg (2 lb) chicken thigh fillets
1 teaspoon salt
1/4 cup (60 ml/2 fl oz) lemon juice
1 cup (250 g/8 oz) yoghurt
1 onion, chopped
2 cloves garlic, crushed
3 cm (1¼ inch) piece ginger, grated
1 green chilli, chopped
3 teaspoons garam masala
2 teaspoons yellow food colouring
1 teaspoon red food colouring
1/2 cup (125 ml/4 fl oz) tomato purée
2 cm (3/4 inch) piece ginger, extra,
    finely grated
1 cup (250 ml/8 fl oz) cream
2 teaspoons sugar
1/4 teaspoon chilli powder
1 tablespoon lemon juice, extra
1 teaspoon ground cumin
100 g (3½ oz) butter

1 Cut the chicken into 2 cm (3/4 inch) thick strips. Sprinkle with the salt and lemon juice.
2 Place the yoghurt, onion, garlic, ginger, chilli and 2 teaspoons of the garam masala in a food processor and blend until smooth.
3 Combine the food colourings in a small bowl. Brush over the chicken and turn the strips to coat the meat all over. Add the yoghurt mixture and toss to combine. Cover and refrigerate for 4 hours. Remove the chicken from the marinade and allow to drain for 5 minutes.
4 Preheat the oven to hot 220°C (425°F/Gas 7). Place the chicken in a shallow baking dish and bake for 15 minutes, or until it is tender. Drain off any excess juice, cover loosely with foil and keep warm.
5 Mix together the tomato purée and 1/2 cup (125 ml/4 fl oz) water in a large jug. Add the ginger, cream, remaining garam marsala, sugar, chilli powder, lemon juice and cumin, and stir to thoroughly combine.
6 Melt the butter in a large pan over medium heat. Stir in the tomato mixture and bring to the boil. Cook for 2 minutes, then reduce the heat and add the chicken pieces. Stir to coat the chicken with the sauce and simmer for a further 2 minutes, or until completely heated through. Serve with rice and garnish with some shredded kaffir lime leaves.

NUTRITION PER SERVE
Protein 55 g; Fat 60 g; Carbohydrate 10 g;
Dietary Fibre 2 g; Cholesterol 330 mg;
3390 kJ (805 Cal)

NOTE: The chicken can also be marinated overnight in the refrigerator. It is important to always use a non-metallic dish when marinating.

HINT: Kaffir lime leaves are available from most supermarkets, Asian food stores and good fruit and vegetable shops.

VARIATION: Chicken pieces can be substituted for the chicken thigh fillets. Score the thickest part of the meat with a knife and then bake for 30–40 minutes, or until tender.

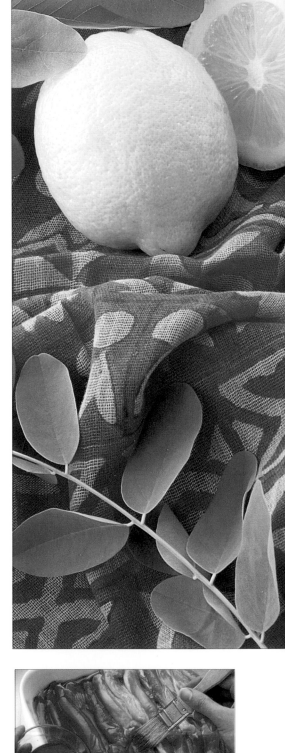

Sprinkle the salt and lemon juice over the strips of chicken.

Process the yoghurt, onion, garlic, ginger, chilli and garam masala.

Brush the food colourings over the chicken, coating the meat thoroughly.

Drain any excess juice from the baked chicken pieces in the baking dish.

Add the ginger, cream, garam masala, sugar, chilli, lemon juice and cumin.

Add the chicken pieces to the pan and stir to coat with the sauce.

MEDITERRANEAN LAMB CASSEROLE

Preparation time: 15 minutes
Total cooking time: 1 hour
Serves 4

1 tablespoon olive oil
750 g (1½ lb) lamb from the bone, diced
1 large onion, sliced
2 cloves garlic, crushed
2 carrots, chopped
2 parsnips, chopped
400 g (13 oz) can chopped tomatoes
2 tablespoons tomato paste
2 teaspoons chopped fresh rosemary
½ cup (125 ml/4 fl oz) red wine
1 cup (250 ml/8 fl oz) chicken stock

1 Heat the oil in large saucepan and cook the lamb, in batches, for 3–4 minutes, or until browned. Remove from the pan and keep warm. Add the onion and garlic to the pan and cook for 2–3 minutes, or until the onion is soft.
2 Return the lamb and juices to the pan. Add the carrots, parsnips, tomatoes, tomato paste, rosemary, wine and stock and bring to the boil. Reduce the heat and cover the pan. Simmer the casserole for 50 minutes, or until the lamb is tender and the sauce has thickened. Serve with soft polenta or couscous.

NUTRITION PER SERVE
Protein 45 g; Fat 12 g; Carbohydrate 12 g; Dietary Fibre 4.5 g; Cholesterol 125 mg; 1517 kJ (362 cal)

Add the onion and garlic to the pan and cook until the onion is soft.

Simmer until the lamb is tender and the sauce has thickened.

CREAMY TOMATO AND CHICKEN STEW

Preparation time: 35 minutes
Total cooking time: 50 minutes
Serves 4–6

4 slices bacon
2 tablespoons oil
50 g (1¾ oz) butter
300 g (10 oz) small button
    mushrooms, halved
1.5 kg (3 lb) chicken pieces
2 onions, chopped
2 cloves garlic, crushed
400 g (13 oz) can tomatoes
1 cup (250 ml/8 fl oz) chicken stock
1 cup (250 ml/8 fl oz) cream
2 tablespoons chopped fresh parsley
2 tablespoons fresh lemon thyme
    leaves

1 Chop the bacon into large pieces. Place a large, heavy-based pan over medium heat. Brown the bacon, then remove and set aside on paper towels.
2 Heat half the oil and a third of the butter in the pan until foaming, then stir in the mushrooms and cook until softened and golden brown. Remove from the pan with a slotted spoon.
3 Add the remaining oil to the pan with a little more butter. When the oil is hot, brown the chicken pieces in batches over high heat until the skin is golden all over and a little crisp. Remove from the pan.
4 Heat the remaining butter in the pan. Add the onion and garlic and cook over medium–high heat for about 3 minutes, or until softened. Pour in the tomatoes, stock and cream. Return the bacon, mushrooms and chicken pieces to the pan and simmer over medium–low heat for 25 minutes.

Stir in the herbs, season to taste with salt and freshly ground black pepper, and simmer the stew for another 5 minutes before serving.

NUTRITION PER SERVE (6)
Protein 70 g; Fat 40 g; Carbohydrate 7 g;
Dietary Fibre 3 g; Cholesterol 215 mg;
2650 kJ (630 Cal)

When the oil and butter are foaming, add the mushrooms and cook until soft.

Brown the chicken pieces in batches over high heat until the skin is golden and crisp.

Add the tomatoes, stock and cream to the softened onion and garlic.

NAVARIN OF LAMB

Preparation time: 20 minutes
Total cooking time: 1 hour 45 minutes
Serves 4

1.25 kg (2 lb 8 oz) boned shoulder or
    leg of lamb (ask your butcher to
    bone the meat)
1 tablespoon oil
1 small onion, quartered
1 clove garlic, crushed
2 rashers bacon, rind removed, finely
    chopped
12 large bulb spring onions, stems
    removed
1 tablespoon plain flour
1 cup (250 ml/8 fl oz) chicken stock
1 tablespoon tomato paste

1 turnip, swede or parsnip, peeled
    and cubed
1 large carrot, thickly sliced
4–6 new potatoes, halved
1/2 cup (60 g/2 oz) frozen peas

1 Remove any excess fat from the
lamb and cut the meat into bite-sized
cubes. Preheat the oven to slow 150°C.
(300°F/Gas 2). Heat the oil in a heavy-
based non-stick frying pan. Cook the
onion, garlic, bacon and spring onions
over medium heat for 5 minutes, or
until the onion is soft. Remove with a
slotted spoon to a large heatproof
casserole dish.
2 Add the lamb to the frying pan and
brown quickly in batches. When all
the meat is browned return it to the
pan and sprinkle with the flour. Stir for

1 minute to combine, then pour on the
stock and tomato paste. Stir until
thickened and smooth and pour into
the casserole.
3 Stir in the turnip, swede or parsnip,
carrot and potato. Cover with a tight-
fitting lid and bake for 1¹/₄ hours,
stirring a couple of times. Add the peas
and cook for another 15 minutes, or
until the lamb is tender. Season to taste
before serving.

NUTRITION PER SERVE
Protein 9 g; Fat 12 g; Carbohydrate 22 g;
Dietary Fibre 7 g; Cholesterol 30 mg;
970 kJ (235 cal)

STORAGE TIME: Keep covered and
refrigerated for up to 3 days.

Remove the onion, spring onion, garlic and
bacon to a casserole dish.

Return all the browned meat to the pan and
sprinkle with flour.

Add the turnip, carrot and potato to the meat in
the casserole dish.

BEEF IN RED WINE

Preparation time: 20 minutes
Total cooking time: 2 hours 15 minutes
Serves 4

2 tablespoons olive oil
1 kg (2 lb) trimmed chuck steak, cubed
12 baby onions, halved, with root base left intact
4 rashers bacon, rind removed, chopped
2 cloves garlic, finely chopped
3 tablespoons plain flour
1½ cups (375 ml/12 fl oz) red wine
2 tablespoons port
2 bay leaves
5 sprigs fresh parsley
3 sprigs fresh thyme
1 thin slice lemon rind
1½ cups (375 ml/12 fl oz) beef or chicken stock
500 g (1 lb) flat mushrooms, halved

1 Heat 1 tablespoon of oil in a large heavy-based pan, and cook the steak in small batches over high heat for 2 minutes, or until well browned. Remove from the pan.
2 Heat the remaining oil in the same pan, and add the onion, bacon and garlic. Stir over medium–high heat for 5 minutes, or until the onion is browned. Return the beef to the pan, add the flour, and stir for 1 minute. Remove the pan from the heat, and gradually stir in the wine and port, mixing the flour in well. Return the pan to the heat and bring to the boil, stirring, then reduce the heat and simmer for 3 minutes, or until the sauce boils and thickens slightly.
3 Make a bouquet garni by wrapping the bay leaves, parsley, thyme and lemon rind in a piece of muslin and tying with string. Add the bouquet garni, stock and mushrooms to the pan, bring to the boil, then reduce the heat to low and simmer, covered, for 2 hours, or until the beef is tender, stirring occasionally. Remove the bouquet garni, and season. Serve with mashed potato and baby carrots.

NUTRITION PER SERVE
Protein 65 g; Fat 20 g; Carbohydrate 12 g; Dietary Fibre 4.5 g; Cholesterol 185 mg; 2332 kJ (557 Cal)

Chop the baby onions in half, leaving the root base intact.

Cook the steak in batches until well browned all over.

Gradually add the wine and port, and stir to mix in the flour.

roasts & bakes

BEEF PIE

Preparation time: 35 minutes + chilling
Total cooking time: 2 hours 30 minutes
Serves 6

FILLING
2 tablespoons oil
1 kg (2 lb) trimmed chuck steak,
    cubed
1 large onion, chopped
1 large carrot, finely chopped
2 cloves garlic, crushed
2 tablespoons plain flour
1 cup (250 ml/8 fl oz) beef stock
2 teaspoons fresh thyme leaves
1 tablespoon Worcestershire sauce

PASTRY
2 cups (250 g/8 oz) plain flour
150 g (5 oz) cold butter, chopped
1 egg yolk
3–4 tablespoons iced water
1 egg yolk and 1 tablespoon milk,
    to glaze

1 Heat 1 tablespoon of the oil in a large pan and cook the meat in batches until browned all over. Remove from the pan and set aside. Heat the remaining oil, then add the onion, carrot and garlic and cook over medium heat until browned.
2 Return the meat to the pan and stir through the flour. Cook for 1 minute, then remove from the heat and slowly stir in the beef stock, mixing the flour in well. Add the thyme leaves and Worcestershire sauce, and bring to the boil. Season to taste with salt and cracked black pepper.
3 Reduce the heat to very low, cover and simmer for 1¹/₂–2 hours, or until the meat is tender. During the last 15 minutes of cooking, remove the lid and allow the liquid to reduce so that the sauce is very thick and suitable for filling a pie. Allow to cool completely.
4 To make the pastry, sift the flour into a large bowl and add the butter. Using your fingertips, rub the butter into the flour until it resembles fine breadcrumbs. Add the egg yolk and 2 tablespoons of iced water, and mix with a knife using a cutting action until the mixture comes together in beads, adding a little more water if necessary. Turn out onto a lightly floured surface and gather together to form a smooth dough. Wrap in plastic wrap and refrigerate for 30 minutes.
5 Preheat the oven to moderately hot 200°C (400°F/Gas 6). Divide the pastry into two pieces and roll out one of the pieces on a sheet of baking paper until large enough to line a 23 cm (9 inch) pie dish. Line the pie dish with the pastry. Fill with the cold filling and roll out the remaining piece of pastry until large enough to fully cover the dish. Dampen the edges of the pastry with your fingers dipped in water. Lay the top piece of pastry over the pie and gently press the bottom and top pieces of pastry together. Trim the overhanging edges with a sharp knife, reroll the scrap pieces to make decorative shapes and press on the pie.
6 Cut a few slits in the top of the pastry to allow the steam to escape. Beat together the egg yolk and milk, and brush it over the top of the pie. Cook in the oven for 20–30 minutes, or until the pastry is golden and the filling is hot.

NUTRITION PER SERVE
Protein 40 g; Fat 35 g; Carbohydrate 35 g;
Dietary Fibre 3 g; Cholesterol 235 mg;
2580 kJ (615 Cal)

Add the butter and rub it into the flour with your fingertips.

Mix the egg yolk and water into the flour mixture with a flat-bladed knife.

Gather the mixture together to form a smooth dough.

The baking paper will help you lift the pastry into the pie dish.

Spoon in the filling then top with the second piece of pastry.

Press the pieces of pastry together and trim off the excess with a sharp knife.

ROAST CHICKEN WITH BREADCRUMB STUFFING

Preparation time: 40 minutes
Total cooking time: 1 hour 30 minutes
Serves 6

3 slices bacon, finely chopped
6 slices wholegrain bread, crusts
    removed
3 spring onions, chopped
2 tablespoons chopped pecans
2 teaspoons currants
1/4 cup (15 g/1/2 oz) finely chopped
    fresh parsley
1 egg, lightly beaten
1/4 cup (60 ml/2 fl oz) milk
1.4 kg (2 lb 13 oz) chicken
40 g (11/4 oz) butter, melted
1 tablespoon oil
1 tablespoon soy sauce
1 clove garlic, crushed
11/2 cups (375 ml/12 fl oz) chicken
    stock
1 tablespoon plain flour

1 Preheat the oven to moderate
180°C (350°F/Gas 4). Cook the bacon
in a dry frying pan over high heat for
5 minutes, or until crisp. Cut the bread
into 1 cm (1/2 inch) cubes and place
in a bowl. Mix in the bacon, spring
onion, pecans, currants, parsley and
combined egg and milk. Season
2 Remove the giblets and any large
amounts of fat from the cavity of the
chicken. Pat the chicken dry with
paper towels. Spoon the bacon
mixture into the chicken cavity. Tuck
the wings under the chicken and tie
the legs securely with string.
3 Place the chicken on a rack in
a deep baking dish. Brush with the
combined butter, oil and soy sauce.
Pour any remaining mixture into the
baking dish with the garlic and half
the stock. Roast the chicken for
1–11/4 hours, or until brown and
tender, basting occasionally with the
pan juices. Pierce between the thigh
and body to the bone and check that
any juices running out are clear. If they
are pink, continue cooking. Put the
chicken on a serving dish. Cover
loosely with foil and leave in a warm
place for 5 minutes before carving.
4 Discard all but 1 tablespoon of the

pan juices from the baking dish.
Transfer the baking dish to the stove.
Add the flour to the pan juices and
blend to a smooth paste. Stir
constantly over low heat for 5 minutes,
or until the mixture browns. Gradually
add the remaining stock and stir until
the mixture boils and thickens. Add a
little extra stock or water if the gravy is

too thick. Season with salt and cracked
black pepper and strain into a jug.
Serve the chicken and gravy with
snow peas and roast potatoes.

NUTRITION PER SERVE
Protein 33 g; Fat 20 g; Carbohydrate 15 g;
Dietary Fibre 3 g; Cholesterol 110 mg;
1530 kJ (365 Cal)

Pat the chicken dry and spoon the stuffing into
the chicken cavity.

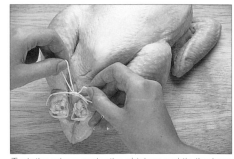

Tuck the wings under the chicken and tie the legs
securely with string.

COTTAGE PIE

Preparation time: 30 minutes
Total cooking time: 1 hour 30 minutes
Serves 6–8

2 tablespoons olive oil
2 onions, chopped
2 carrots, diced
1 celery stick, diced
1 kg (2 lb) beef mince
2 tablespoons plain flour
1¹/₂ cups (375 ml/12 fl oz) beef stock
1 tablespoon soy sauce
1 tablespoon Worcestershire sauce
2 tablespoons tomato sauce
1 tablespoon tomato paste
2 bay leaves
2 teaspoons chopped fresh flat-leaf
	parsley

TOPPING
800 g (1 lb 10 oz) potatoes, diced
400 g (13 oz) parsnips, diced
30 g (1 oz) butter
¹/₂ cup (125 ml/4 fl oz) milk

1 Heat the oil in a large frying pan over medium heat and cook the onion, carrot and celery, stirring occasionally, for 5 minutes, or until softened and lightly coloured. Add the mince and cook for 7 minutes, then stir in the flour and cook for 2 minutes. Add the stock, soy sauce, Worcestershire sauce, tomato sauce, tomato paste and bay leaves and simmer over low heat for 30 minutes, stirring occasionally. Leave to cool. Remove the bay leaves and stir in the parsley.
2 To make the topping, boil the potato and parsnip in salted water for 15–20 minutes, or until cooked through. Drain, return to the pan and mash with the butter and enough of the milk to make a firm mash.
3 Preheat the oven to 180°C (350°F/ Gas 4) and lightly grease a 2.5 litre ovenproof dish. Spoon the filling into the dish and spread the topping over it. Fluff with a fork. Bake for 25 minutes, or until golden.

NUTRITION PER SERVE (8)
Protein 31 g; Fat 18 g; Carbohydrate 27 g; Dietary Fibre 4 g; Cholesterol 78 mg; 1640 kJ (390 Cal)

Mash the potato and parsnip together with a potato masher.

Spoon the cooled meat filling into the lightly greased dish.

QUICHE LORRAINE

Preparation time: 35 minutes + chilling
Total cooking time: 1 hour 5 minutes
Serves 6

1¼ cups (155 g/5 oz) plain flour
90 g (3 oz) cold butter, chopped
2–3 tablespoons iced water
4 rashers bacon, rind removed
75 g (2½ oz) Gruyère, finely grated
3 eggs
½ cup (125 ml/4 fl oz) cream
½ cup (125 ml/4 fl oz) milk

1 Sift the flour into a bowl and rub in the butter with your fingertips until the mixture resembles fine breadcrumbs. Make a well in the centre and add the water. Using a cutting action, mix with a flat-bladed knife until the mixture comes together in beads. Gently gather the dough together and lift onto a floured surface. Press into a ball and flatten it slightly. Wrap in plastic wrap and refrigerate for 15 minutes. Preheat the oven to moderately hot 200°C (400°F/Gas 6).

2 Roll the dough out between two sheets of baking paper until large enough to line a 23 cm (9 inch) fluted flan tin. Remove the top sheet of paper and invert the pastry into the tin (draping it over the rolling pin may help). Use a small ball of pastry to help press the pastry into the tin, leaving any excess to hang over the side. Roll the rolling pin over the tin to cut off any excess, and then refrigerate for 15 minutes.

3 Line the pastry shell with enough crumpled greaseproof paper to cover the base and side of the tin. Pour in some baking beads and bake for 15 minutes. Remove the paper and beads and return the pastry to the oven for 10 minutes, or until the base is dry. Cool completely before filling. Reduce the oven to moderate 180°C (350°F/Gas 4).

4 Cut the bacon into short, thin strips and cook in a frying pan until brown and crisp. Drain, then spread evenly over the pastry base. Sprinkle the cheese over the bacon. In a jug, whisk together the eggs, cream and milk. Stand the tin on a baking tray, and pour the egg mixture into the pastry shell. Bake for 35–40 minutes, or until set and lightly golden.

NUTRITION PER SERVE
Protein 15 g; Fat 28 g; Carbohydrate 20 g;
Dietary Fibre 1 g; Cholesterol 180 mg;
1640 kJ (390 Cal)

Add the water and mix together with a flat-bladed knife.

Roll out the dough until it is large enough to line the tin.

Remove any excess pastry by rolling a rolling pin over the top of the tin.

MEATLOAF

Preparation time: 25 minutes
Total cooking time: 1 hour 15 minutes
Serves 6

125 g (4 oz) bacon, trimmed and
    chopped
500 g (1 lb) beef mince
500 g (1 lb) pork mince
1 onion, coarsely grated
2 cloves garlic, crushed
2 cups (160 g/5¹/₂ oz) fresh
    breadcrumbs
2 teaspoons fresh thyme leaves
1 egg, lightly beaten
1 tablespoon red wine vinegar
2 teaspoons soft brown sugar

1 Preheat the oven to moderate 180°C
(350°F/Gas 4). Lightly grease a loaf tin
then line with a single sheet of baking
paper, leaving the paper to overhang
on the long sides of the tin.
2 Heat a non-stick frying pan, add
the chopped bacon, and cook, stirring,
until crispy. Drain on paper towels.
3 Place the mince, onion, garlic,
breadcrumbs, thyme, egg, vinegar,
sugar and bacon in a bowl. Season
and combine, using your hands. Don't
overmix or the meatloaf will become
too dense when cooked.
4 Spoon the mixture into the loaf tin
and press down gently. Smooth the
top and cook in the oven for 1 hour
10 minutes, or until browned and
cooked through. Test if it is cooked by
pushing a metal skewer or sharp knife
into the centre, leaving it for 3 seconds,
and then pulling it out and holding it
against your wrist. If it is really hot, it
is cooked through; if not, cook a little
longer. Leave for 5 minutes and pour
the cooking juices into a jug. Lift out
the meatloaf using the overhanging
baking paper. Cut into slices with a
serrated knife and drizzle with the
cooking juices. Serve with tomato
sauce, peas, corn and potatoes.

NUTRITION PER SERVE
Protein 45 g; Fat 13 g; Carbohydrate 20 g;
Dietary Fibre 1.5 g; Cholesterol 135 mg;
1588 kJ (380 Cal)

Line the tin with baking paper, allowing it to
overhang the long sides of the tin.

Spoon the mixture into the tin and gently press
down with the back of a spoon.

ROAST LEG OF PORK

Preparation time: 30 minutes
Total cooking time: 3 hours 45 minutes
Serves 8

4 kg (8 lb) leg of pork
oil and salt, to rub on pork

GRAVY
1 tablespoon brandy or Calvados
2 tablespoons plain flour
1½ cups (375 ml/12 fl oz) chicken
 stock
½ cup (125 ml/4 fl oz) unsweetened
 apple juice

1 Preheat the oven to very hot 250°C (500°F/Gas 10). Score the rind of the pork with a sharp knife at 2 cm (3/4 inch) intervals. Rub in some oil and salt to ensure crisp crackling. Place the pork, rind-side-up, on a rack in a large baking dish.

2 Add a little water to the dish. Roast for 30 minutes, or until the rind begins to crackle and bubble. Reduce the heat to moderate 180°C (350°F/Gas 4). Roast for 2 hours 40 minutes (20 minutes per 500 g/1 lb) then roast for a further 30 minutes. The pork is cooked if the juices run clear when the flesh is pierced with a skewer. Do not cover the pork or the crackling will soften. Leave in a warm place for 10 minutes.

3 To make the gravy, drain off all except 2 tablespoons of the pan juices from the baking dish. Place on top of the stove over moderate heat, add the brandy and stir quickly to lift the sediment from the bottom of the pan. Cook for 1 minute. Remove from the heat, stir in the flour and mix well. Return the pan to the heat and cook for 2 minutes, stirring constantly. Gradually add the stock and apple juice, and cook, stirring constantly, until the gravy boils and thickens. Season to taste with salt and cracked pepper. Slice the pork and serve with the crackling, gravy, apple sauce and baked apple wedges and vegetables.

NUTRITION PER SERVE
Protein 157 g; Fat 8.5 g; Carbohydrate 2.4 g; Dietary Fibre 0 g; Cholesterol 305 mg; 3050 kJ (730 Cal)

NOTE: Cook the pork just before serving. Any leftover pork can be refrigerated, covered, for up to 3 days.

Use a sharp knife to score the pork rind at regular intervals.

Rub oil and salt into the rind to make sure the crackling will be crisp.

Test the pork by piercing with a skewer—if the juices run clear, the flesh is cooked.

STEAK AND KIDNEY PUDDING

Preparation time: 25 minutes
Total cooking time: 5 hours
Serves 4

2³/₄ cups (340 g/11 oz) self-raising
    flour
150 g (5 oz) butter, frozen and grated
700 g (1 lb 7 oz) chuck steak, cut into
    2 cm (³/₄ inch) pieces
200 g (6¹/₂ oz) ox kidney, cleaned and
    cut into 2 cm (³/₄ inch) pieces
1 small onion, finely chopped
2 teaspoons finely chopped fresh
    parsley
1 tablespoon plain flour
1 teaspoon Worcestershire sauce
³/₄ cup (185 ml/6 fl oz) beef stock

1 Grease a 1.5 litre pudding basin with melted butter, and put a round of baking paper in the bottom. Place the empty basin in a large pan on a trivet or upturned saucer and pour in enough cold water to come halfway up the side of the basin. Remove the basin and put the water on to boil.
2 Sift the flour into a bowl and add the butter and a large pinch of salt. Mix together with a flat-bladed knife and add enough water to form a soft dough. Reserve one-third of the dough and roll the rest out to a circle about 1 cm (³/₄ inch) thick. Sprinkle with flour and fold it in half. Using a rolling pin, roll the straight edge away from you, making sure the two halves don't stick together—this helps form a bag shape. Fit the bag into the pudding basin and stretch it to fit, leaving a little hanging over the edge, and brush out any excess flour.
3 Mix the steak, kidney, onion,

parsley and flour together in a bowl. Season and add the Worcestershire sauce. Put the mixture into the pastry case and add enough stock or water to come three-quarters of the way up the meat. Roll out the remaining pastry to form a lid the same size as the top of the bowl. Fold overhanging pastry into the bowl and dampen the edge with water. Put the lid on and press the edges together securely.
4 Lay a sheet of foil then a sheet of baking paper on the work surface, and make a large pleat in the middle. Grease with melted butter. Place

paper-side-down across the top of the basin and tie string securely around the rim and over the top of the basin to make a handle. This is used to lift the pudding in and out of the pan.
5 Lower the basin into the simmering water and cover with a tight-fitting lid. Cook for 5 hours, checking every hour and topping up with boiling water as needed. Serve from the basin.

NUTRITION PER SERVE
Protein 55 g; Fat 40 g; Carbohydrate 63 g; Dietary Fibre 3.7 g; Cholesterol 370 mg; 3402 kJ (813 Cal)

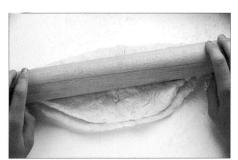

Roll the straight edge away from you to form a bag shape.

Fit the bag into the basin, leaving a little pastry hanging over the edge.

Pour in enough stock or water to come three-quarters of the way up the meat.

CHICKEN PIES

Preparation time: 50 minutes
  + 30 minutes refrigeration
Total cooking time: 1 hour
Serves 4

300 g (10 oz) chicken breast fillet
1 bay leaf
2 cups (500 ml/16 oz) chicken stock
2 large potatoes, chopped
250 g (8 oz) orange sweet potato,
    chopped
2 celery sticks, chopped
2 carrots, chopped
1 onion, chopped
1 parsnip, chopped
1 clove garlic, crushed
1 tablespoon cornflour
1 cup (250 ml/8 fl oz) skim milk
1 cup (155 g/5 oz) frozen peas,
    thawed
1 tablespoon chopped fresh chives
1 tablespoon chopped fresh parsley
1 1/2 cups (185 g/6 oz) self-raising flour
20 g (3/4 oz) butter
1/3 cup (80 ml/2 3/4 fl oz) milk
1 egg, lightly beaten
1/2 teaspoon sesame seeds

1 Combine the chicken, bay leaf and stock in a large, deep non-stick frying pan and simmer over low heat for about 10 minutes until the chicken is cooked through. Remove the chicken, set aside and, when cool, cut into small pieces. Add the chopped potato, orange sweet potato, celery and carrot to the pan and simmer, covered, for about 10 minutes, until just tender. Remove the vegetables from the pan with a slotted spoon.
2 Add the onion, parsnip and garlic to the pan and simmer, uncovered, for about 10 minutes, until very soft.

Discard the bay leaf. Purée in a food processor until smooth.
3 Stir the cornflour into 2 tablespoons of the skim milk until it forms a smooth paste, stir into the puréed mixture with the remaining milk and then return to the pan. Stir over low heat until the mixture boils and thickens. Preheat the oven to moderately hot 200°C (400°F/Gas 6).
4 Combine the puréed mixture with the remaining vegetables, chicken and herbs. Season with salt and pepper. Spoon into four 1 3/4 cup (440 ml/ 14 fl oz) capacity ovenproof dishes.
5 To make the pastry, sift the flour into a large bowl, rub in the butter with your fingertips, then make a well in the centre. Combine the milk with 1/3 cup (80 ml/2 3/4 fl oz) water and add enough to the dry ingredients to make a soft dough. Turn out onto a lightly floured surface and knead until just smooth. Cut the dough into four portions and roll each out so that it is 1 cm (1/2 inch) larger than the top of the dish. Brush the edge of the dough with some of the egg and fit over the top of each dish, pressing the edge firmly to seal.
6 Brush the pastry tops lightly with beaten egg and sprinkle with the sesame seeds. Bake for about 30 minutes, until the tops are golden and the filling is heated through.

NUTRITION PER SERVE
Protein 30 g; Fat 10 g; Carbohydrate 65 g; Dietary Fibre 9.5 g; Cholesterol 100 mg; 2045 kJ (490 cal)

Cut the vegetables into even-sized pieces so that they cook at the same rate.

Simmer the chicken and bay leaf in the stock until the chicken is cooked through.

Purée the cooked onion, parsnip and garlic together until smooth.

Stir the sauce constantly until the mixture boils and thickens.

Add enough liquid to the dry ingredients to make a soft dough.

Brush the edge of the dough with egg, then press over the top of each dish.

MOUSSAKA

Preparation time: 30 minutes
Total cooking time: 1 hour 30 minutes
Serves 6

1 kg (2 lb) eggplants
cooking oil spray
400 g (13 oz) lean lamb mince
2 onions, finely chopped
2 cloves garlic, crushed
400 g (13 oz) can tomatoes
1 tablespoon chopped fresh thyme
1 teaspoon chopped fresh oregano
1 tablespoon tomato paste
$^1/_3$ cup (80 ml/$2^3/_4$ fl oz) dry white
 wine
1 bay leaf
1 teaspoon sugar

CHEESE SAUCE
$1^1/_4$ cups (315 ml/10 fl oz) skim milk
2 tablespoons plain flour
$^1/_4$ cup (30 g/1 oz) grated reduced-fat
 Cheddar
1 cup (250 g/8 oz) ricotta
pinch of cayenne pepper
$^1/_4$ teaspoon ground nutmeg

1 Cut the eggplant into 1 cm ($^1/_2$ inch) thick slices, place in a colander over a large bowl, layering with a generous sprinkling of salt, and leave to stand for 20 minutes. This is to draw out the bitter juices.
2 Lightly spray a non-stick frying pan with oil and brown the lamb mince, in batches if necessary, over medium-high heat. Once all the meat is browned, set aside.
3 Spray the pan again with oil, add the onion and stir continuously for 2 minutes. Add 1 tablespoon water to the pan to prevent sticking. Add the garlic and cook for about 3 minutes, or

until the onion is golden brown.
4 Push the undrained tomatoes through a sieve, then discard the contents of the sieve.
5 Return the meat to the pan with the onion. Add the herbs, tomato pulp, tomato paste, wine, bay leaf and sugar. Cover and simmer over low heat for 20 minutes. Preheat a grill.
6 Thoroughly rinse and pat dry the eggplant, place on a grill tray, spray lightly with oil and grill under high heat until golden brown. Turn over, spray lightly with oil and grill until golden brown. Arrange half the eggplant slices over the base of a 1.5 litre capacity baking dish. Top with half the meat mixture and then repeat the layers.
7 Preheat the oven to moderate 180°C (350°F/Gas 4). To make the cheese sauce, blend a little of the milk with the flour to form a paste in a small pan. Gradually blend in the remaining milk, stirring constantly over low heat until the milk starts to simmer and thicken. Remove from the heat and stir in the Cheddar, ricotta, cayenne and nutmeg. Pour over the moussaka and bake for 35–40 minutes, or until the cheese is golden brown and the moussaka heated through.

NUTRITION PER SERVE
Protein 10 g; Fat 10 g; Carbohydrate 15 g; Dietary Fibre 5.5 g; Cholesterol 25 mg; 735 kJ (175 cal)

STORAGE TIME: Freeze for up to 2 months. Thaw in the fridge, then heat in a moderate oven for 30–45 minutes.

Sprinkle a generous amount of salt on the eggplant slices and set aside.

Empty the can of tomatoes into a sieve and push the tomatoes through.

Stir the herbs, tomato pulp, tomato paste, wine, bay leaf and sugar into the meat.

Rinse and dry the eggplant slices and grill on both sides until golden.

Layer the eggplant slices and meat evenly in the baking dish.

Remove from the heat before adding the Cheddar, ricotta, cayenne and nutmeg.

FAMILY-STYLE MEAT PIE

Preparation time: 30 minutes + cooling
  + 20 minutes refrigeration
Total cooking time: 1 hour 45 minutes
Serves 6

1 tablespoon oil
1 onion, chopped
1 clove garlic, crushed
750 g (1 lb 8 oz) beef mince
1 cup (250 ml/8 fl oz) beef stock
1 cup (250 ml/8 fl oz) beer
1 tablespoon tomato paste
1 tablespoon vegetable yeast extract
1 tablespoon Worcestershire sauce
2 teaspoons cornflour
375 g (12 oz) shortcrust pastry
375 g (12 oz) puff pastry
1 egg, lightly beaten

1 Heat the oil in a large saucepan over medium heat, add the onion and cook for 5 minutes, or until golden. Increase the heat to high, add the garlic and mince and cook, breaking up any lumps, for about 5 minutes, or until the mince changes colour.
2 Add the stock, beer, tomato paste, yeast extract, Worcestershire sauce and ½ cup (125 ml/4 fl oz) water. Reduce the heat to medium and cook for

1 hour, or until there is little liquid left. Combine the cornflour with 1 tablespoon water, then stir into the mince and cook for 5 minutes, or until the mixture is thick and glossy. Remove from the heat and leave to cool completely.
3 Lightly grease a 23 cm (9 inch) top, 18 cm (7 inch) base, 3 cm (1¼ inch) deep pie tin. Roll the shortcrust pastry out between two sheets of baking paper until it is large enough to line the base and side of the tin. Remove the top sheet of paper and invert the pastry into the tin, then remove the remaining sheet of paper. Use a ball of pastry to help press the pastry into the tin, allowing any excess to hang over.
4 Roll out the puff pastry between two sheets of baking paper to a 24 cm (9½ inch) circle. Spoon the cooled

filling into the pastry shell and smooth it down. Brush the pastry edges with beaten egg, then place the puff pastry over the top. Cut off any overhang with a sharp knife. Press the top and bottom pastries together, then scallop the edges with a fork or your fingers, and refrigerate for 20 minutes. Preheat the oven to moderately hot 200°C (400°F/Gas 6) and heat a baking tray.
5 Brush the remaining egg over the top of the pie, place on the hot tray on the bottom shelf of the oven (this helps make a crisp crust for this pie) and bake for 25–30 minutes, or until the pastry is golden and well puffed.

NUTRITION PER SERVE
Protein 38 g; Fat 43.5 g; Carbohydrate 52 g; Dietary Fibre 2.5 g; Cholesterol 129.5 mg; 3120 kJ (745 Cal)

Spoon the cooled meat filling evenly into the pastry shell.

Trim the edges of the puff pastry with a very sharp knife.

SALMON AND SPRING ONION QUICHE

Preparation time: 20 minutes +
   20 minutes refrigeration
Total cooking time: 1 hour
Serves 6

2 cups (250 g/8 oz) self-raising flour
150 g (5 oz) butter, melted
1/2 cup (125 ml/4 fl oz) milk

FILLING
425 g (14 oz) can red salmon, drained
   and flaked
4 spring onions, sliced
1/3 cup (20 g/3/4 oz) chopped fresh
   parsley
4 eggs, lightly beaten
1/2 cup (125 ml/4 fl oz) milk
1/2 cup (125 ml/4 fl oz) cream
1/2 cup (60 g/2 oz) grated Cheddar

1 Grease a 26 cm (10 1/2 inch) loose-based fluted tart tin. Sift the flour into a large bowl and make a well in the centre. Pour in the melted butter and milk and mix until the mixture comes together and forms a dough. Refrigerate for 20 minutes. Preheat the oven to 200°C (400°F/Gas 6). Roll out the pastry and line the tin, trimming away the excess.

2 Cover the pastry with baking paper and spread with a layer of baking beads or rice. Bake for 15 minutes. Remove the paper and beads and bake for 10 minutes. Cool. Reduce the oven to 180°C (350°F/Gas 4).

3 Place the salmon in the pastry shell. Mix together the spring onions, parsley, eggs, milk, cream and cheese and pour into the pastry shell. Bake for 30 minutes, or until set.

NUTRITION PER SERVE
Protein 20 g; Fat 35 g; Carbohydrate 20 g;
Dietary Fibre 1 g; Cholesterol 210 mg;
1985 kJ (470 cal)

Break the drained canned red salmon into flakes with a fork.

Pour the melted butter and milk into the well in the sifted flour.

Mix together the spring onions, parsley, eggs, milk, cream and cheese.

TRADITIONAL ROAST BEEF WITH YORKSHIRE PUDDINGS

Preparation time: 15 minutes
Total cooking time: 1 hour 45 minutes
Serves 6

2.5 kg (5 lb) piece roasting beef
2 cloves garlic, crushed
1 tablepoon plain flour
2 tablespoons red wine
1¼ cups (315 ml/10 fl oz) beef stock

YORKSHIRE PUDDINGS
2 cups (250 g/8 oz) plain flour
4 eggs
400 ml (13 fl oz) milk

1 Preheat the oven to very hot 240°C (475°F/Gas 9). Rub the outside of the beef with garlic and cracked black pepper. Place on a rack in a baking dish, and roast for 15 minutes.
2 To make the Yorkshire puddings, sift the flour and a pinch of salt into a bowl, and make a well in the centre. Add the eggs and whisk. Gradually pour in the milk and whisk to a smooth batter. Pour into a jug, cover and leave for about 30 minutes.
3 Reduce the heat to moderate 180°C (350°F/Gas 4), and roast the meat for 50–60 minutes for a rare result, or a little longer for well done. Cover the meat loosely with foil and leave in a warm place for 10–15 minutes. Increase the oven temperature to hot 220°C (425°F/Gas 7).
4 Pour the pan juices into a jug, then separate the oil from the meat juices, reserving both. Put 1 teaspoon of the oil in each hole of a 12-hole, deep patty pan (if there is not enough of the oil, use vegetable oil). Heat in the oven for 2–3 minutes, or until just smoking. Pour in the pudding batter to three-quarters full, return to the oven and bake for 5 minutes. Reduce the oven to moderately hot 200°C (400°F/Gas 6) and bake for 10 minutes, or until risen, crisp and golden.
5 Meanwhile, put the baking dish with the reserved meat juices on the stove over low heat. Add the flour and stir, scraping the bottom of the pan to release any sediment. Cook over medium heat, stirring constantly, until the flour is browned. Combine the wine and stock, and gradually stir into the flour mixture. Cook, stirring constantly, until the gravy boils and thickens. Simmer for 3 minutes.
6 Serve the sliced roast beef on a warm plate with the gravy, hot Yorkshire puddings, Brussels sprouts and roast potatoes.

NUTRITION PER SERVE
Protein 100 g; Fat 20 g; Carbohydrate 35 g; Dietary Fibre 2 g; Cholesterol 335 mg; 3085 kJ (740 Cal)

NOTE: Cuts of beef suitable for this recipe include rib eye roast, rump or Scotch fillet.

Rub garlic over the outside of the meat and season with cracked pepper.

Pour the pan juices into a jug and allow the oil to separate from the meat juices.

Pour the pudding batter into the holes until three-quarters full.

BACON AND EGG PIE

Preparation time: 20 minutes + chilling
Total cooking time: 1 hour
Serves 4–6

1 sheet shortcrust pastry
2 teaspoons oil
4 rashers bacon, chopped
5 eggs, lightly beaten
1/4 cup (60 ml/2 fl oz) cream
1 sheet puff pastry
1 egg, extra, lightly beaten, to glaze

1 Preheat the oven to 210°C (415°F/ Gas 6–7). Lightly oil a 20 cm (8 inch) loose-bottomed flan tin. Place the shortcrust pastry in the tin and trim the pastry edges. Cut a sheet of greaseproof paper to cover the pastry-lined tin. Spread a layer of baking beads, dried beans or rice over the paper. Bake for 10 minutes and then discard the paper and rice. Bake the pastry for another 5–10 minutes or until golden. Allow to cool.
2 Heat the oil in a frying pan. Add the bacon and cook over medium heat for a few minutes or until lightly browned. Drain on paper towels and allow to cool slightly. Arrange the bacon over the pastry base and pour the mixed eggs and cream over the top.
3 Brush the edges of the pastry with the egg glaze, cover with puff pastry and press on firmly to seal. Trim the pastry edges and decorate the top with trimmings. Brush with egg glaze and bake for 30–35 minutes, or until puffed and golden.

NUTRITION PER SERVE (6)
Protein 14 g; Fat 26 g; Carbohydrate 23 g;
Dietary Fibre 1 g; Cholesterol 215 mg;
1569 kJ (375 cal)

Spread a layer of dried beans or rice over the paper before blind baking.

Carefully pour the combined eggs and cream over the top of the bacon.

GARLIC PRAWNS

Preparation time: 20 minutes
Total cooking time: 15 minutes
Serves 4

1.25 kg (2½ lb) raw prawns, peeled,
  tails intact, deveined
80 g (2¾ oz) butter, melted
¾ cup (185 ml/6 fl oz) olive oil
8 cloves garlic, crushed
2 spring onions, thinly sliced

1 Preheat the oven to very hot 250°C (500°F/Gas 10). Cut a slit down the back of each prawn.
2 Combine the butter and oil and divide among four 2 cup (500 ml/16 fl oz) cast iron pots. Divide half the crushed garlic among the pots.
3 Place the pots on a baking tray and heat in the oven for 10 minutes, or until the mixture is bubbling. Remove and divide the prawns and remaining garlic among the pots. Return to the oven for 5 minutes, or until the prawns

are cooked. Stir in the spring onion. Season, to taste. Serve with crusty bread to mop up the juices.

NUTRITION PER SERVE
Protein 20 g; Fat 61 g; Carbohydrate 1 g;
Dietary Fibre 1 g; Cholesterol 192.5 mg;
2620 kJ (625 Cal)

NOTE: This is the traditional way to make garlic prawns but they can be successfully made in a cast iron frying pan in the oven or on the stovetop.

Carefully cut a slit down the back of each prawn with a sharp knife.

When the mixture in the pots is bubbling, remove from the oven.

Divide the prawns and remaining crushed garlic among the pots.

MUSTARD CHICKEN AND ASPARAGUS QUICHE

Preparation time: 25 minutes
  + 40 minutes refrigeration
Total cooking time: 1 hour 20 minutes
Serves 8

2 cups (250 g/8 oz) plain flour
100 g (3½ oz) cold butter, chopped
1 egg yolk

FILLING
150 g (5 oz) asparagus, chopped
25 g (¾ oz) butter
1 onion, chopped
¼ cup (60 g/2 oz) wholegrain
    mustard
200 g (6½ oz) soft cream cheese
½ cup (125 ml/4 fl oz) cream
3 eggs, lightly beaten
200 g (6½ oz) cooked chicken,
    chopped
½ teaspoon black pepper

1 Process the flour and butter until crumbly. Add the egg yolk and ¼ cup (60 ml/2 fl oz) of water. Process in short bursts until the mixture comes together. Add a little extra water if needed. Turn onto a floured surface and gather into a ball. Cover with plastic wrap and chill for 30 minutes. Grease a deep loose-based flan tin measuring 19 cm (7½ inches) across the base.
2 Roll out the pastry and line the tin. Trim off any excess with a sharp knife. Place the flan tin on a baking tray and chill for 10 minutes. Preheat the oven to moderately hot 200°C (400°F/Gas 6). Cover the pastry with baking paper and fill evenly with baking beads. Bake for 10 minutes. Remove the paper and beads and bake for about

10 minutes, or until the pastry is lightly browned and dry. Cool. Reduce the oven to moderate 180°C (350°F/Gas 4).
3 To make the filling, boil or steam the asparagus until tender. Drain and pat dry with paper towels. Heat the butter in a pan and cook the onion until translucent. Remove from the heat and add the mustard and cream cheese, stirring until the cheese has melted. Cool. Add the cream, eggs,

chicken and asparagus and mix well.
4 Spoon the filling into the pastry shell and sprinkle with the pepper. Bake for 50 minutes to 1 hour, or until puffed and set. Cool for at least 15 minutes before cutting.

NUTRITION PER SERVE
Protein 15 g; Fat 30 g; Carbohydrate 25 g;
Dietary Fibre 2 g; Cholesterol 190 mg;
1860 kJ (440 Cal)

When the flour and butter mixture is crumbly, add the egg yolk.

Dry the asparagus well to prevent excess moisture from softening the quiche.

Add the mustard and cream cheese and stir until the cheese has melted.

FISH PIE

Preparation time: 10 minutes
Total cooking time: 45 minutes
Serves 4

2 large potatoes (500 g/1 lb), chopped
1/4 cup (60 ml/2 fl oz) milk or cream
1 egg
60 g (2 oz) butter
1/2 cup (60 g/2 oz) grated Cheddar
800 g (1 lb 10 oz) white fish fillets,
    cut into large chunks
1 1/2 cups (375 ml/12 fl oz) milk
1 onion, finely chopped
1 clove garlic, crushed
2 tablespoons plain flour
2 tablespoons lemon juice
2 teaspoons lemon rind
1 tablespoon chopped fresh dill

1 Preheat the oven to moderate 180°C (350°F/Gas 4). Boil or steam the potatoes until tender. Drain and mash well with the milk or cream, egg and half the butter. Mix in half the cheese, then set aside and keep warm.
2 Put the fish in a shallow frying pan and cover with the milk. Bring to the boil, then reduce the heat and simmer for 2–3 minutes, or until the fish flakes when tested with a knife. Drain the fish well, reserving the milk, and set aside.
3 Melt the remaining butter over medium heat in a pan and cook the onion and garlic for 2 minutes. Stir in the flour and cook for 1 minute, or until pale and foaming. Remove from the heat and gradually stir in the reserved milk. Return to the heat and stir constantly until the sauce boils and thickens. Reduce the heat and simmer for 2 minutes. Add the lemon juice, lemon rind and dill, and season.
4 Put the fish into a 1.5 litre ovenproof dish and gently mix in the sauce. Spoon the potato over the fish and top with the remaining cheese. Bake in the oven for 35 minutes, or until the top is browned.

NUTRITION PER SERVE
Protein 55 g; Fat 30 g; Carbohydrate 25 g; Dietary Fibre 3 g; Cholesterol 255 mg; 2460 kJ (585 Cal)

Use a potato masher to mash the potatoes with the milk or cream, egg and butter.

Put the pieces of fish in a frying pan and cover with the milk.

Put spoonfuls of the potato mixture on top of the fish.

TUNA MORNAY

Preparation time: 20 minutes
Total cooking time: 25 minutes
Serves 4

60 g (2 oz) butter
2 tablespoons plain flour
2 cups (500 ml/16 fl oz) milk
1/2 teaspoon dry mustard
3/4 cup (90 g/3 oz) grated Cheddar
425 g (14 oz) can tuna in brine,
    drained
180 g (6 oz) can tuna in brine, drained
2 tablespoons finely chopped fresh
    parsley
2 eggs, hard boiled and chopped
1/3 cup (25 g/3/4 oz) fresh breadcrumbs
paprika, to season

1 Preheat the oven to moderate 180°C (350°F/Gas 4). Melt the butter in a small pan, then add the flour and stir over low heat for 1 minute. Remove the pan from the heat and add the milk gradually, stirring until smooth between each addition.
2 Return the pan to the heat and stir constantly until the sauce boils and thickens. Reduce the heat and simmer for 2 minutes. Remove from the heat, whisk in the mustard and 1/2 cup (60 g/ 2 oz) cheese until melted and smooth.
3 Flake the tuna with a fork, and mix into the sauce, along with the parsley and egg. Season with salt and pepper. Spoon the mixture into four 1-cup (250 ml/8 fl oz) ovenproof ramekins. Mix together the breadcrumbs and remaining cheese and sprinkle over the mornay. Dust very lightly with paprika. Bake for 15–20 minutes, or until the topping is golden brown.

NUTRITION PER SERVE
Protein 55 g; Fat 30 g; Carbohydrate 15 g; Dietary Fibre 0.5 g; Cholesterol 260 mg; 2320 kJ (555 Cal)

Gradually add the milk, stirring until smooth between each addition.

Use a fork to flake the tuna, then stir it into the sauce.

CORNISH PASTIES

Preparation time: 1 hour + chilling
Total cooking time: 45 minutes
Makes 6

2¹/₂ cups (310 g/10 oz) plain flour
125 g (4 oz) butter, chilled and cubed
4–5 tablespoons iced water
160 g (5¹/₂ oz) round steak, diced
1 small potato, finely chopped
1 small onion, finely chopped
1 small carrot, finely chopped
1–2 teaspoons Worcestershire sauce
2 tablespoons beef stock
1 egg, lightly beaten

1 Grease a baking tray. Mix the flour, butter and a pinch of salt in a food processor for 15 seconds, or until crumbly. Add the water and process in short bursts until it comes together. Turn out onto a floured surface and form into a ball. Wrap in plastic and chill for 30 minutes. Preheat the oven to 210°C (415°F/Gas 6–7).

2 Mix together the steak, potato, onion, carrot, Worcestershire sauce and stock. Season well.

3 Divide the dough into six portions and roll out to 3 mm (¹/₈ inch) thick. Cut into six 16 cm (6¹/₂ inch) rounds. Divide the filling evenly and put in the centre of each pastry circle.

4 Brush the pastry edges with egg and fold over. Pinch to form a frill and place on the tray. Brush with egg and bake for 15 minutes. Lower the heat to 180°C (350°F/Gas 4) and bake for 25–30 minutes, or until golden.

NUTRITION PER PASTY
Protein 15 g; Fat 20 g; Carbohydrate 40 g;
Dietary Fibre 3 g; Cholesterol 100 mg;
1665 kJ (395 cal)

Process the flour, butter and salt until the mixture resembles fine breadcrumbs.

Mix together the steak, potato, onion, carrot, Worcestershire sauce and stock.

Fold the pastry over the filling to form a semi-circle and pinch to close.

POTATO GRATIN

Preparation time: 25 minutes
Total cooking time: 1 hour 5 minutes
Serves 4

30 g (1 oz) butter
1 onion, halved and thinly sliced
650 g (1 lb 5 oz) floury potatoes,
   thinly sliced
2/3 cup (90 g/3 oz) grated Cheddar
300 ml (10 fl oz) cream
100 ml (3 1/2 fl oz) milk

1 Heat the butter in a frying pan and cook the onion over low heat for 5 minutes, or until it is soft and translucent.

2 Preheat the oven to warm 160°C (315°F/Gas 3). Grease the base and sides of a deep 1 litre ovenproof dish. Layer the potato slices with the onion and cheese (reserving 2 tablespoons of cheese for the top). Whisk together the cream and milk, and season with salt and cracked black pepper. Slowly pour over the potato, then sprinkle with the remaining cheese.

3 Bake for 50–60 minutes, or until golden brown and the potato is very soft. Leave to rest for 10 minutes before serving.

NUTRITION PER SERVE
Protein 12 g; Fat 50 g; Carbohydrate 25 g;
Dietary Fibre 3 g; Cholesterol 155 mg;
2465 kJ (590 Cal)

VARIATION: For something different, try combining potato and orange sweet potato, layering alternately. For extra flavour, add chopped fresh herbs to the cream and milk mixture.

Peel the onion and slice it in half before cutting into thin slices.

Use a large sharp knife to cut the potatoes into thin slices.

Add the onion to the butter and cook until soft and translucent.

115

CHICKEN AND LEEK COBBLER

Preparation time: 1 hour
Total cooking time: 1 hour
Serves 4–6

50 g (1³/₄ oz) butter
1 kg (2 lb) chicken breast fillets, cut into thick strips
1 large (225 g/7 oz) leek, trimmed and thinly sliced
1 celery stick, thinly sliced
1 tablespoon plain flour
1 cup (250 ml/8 fl oz) chicken stock
1 cup (250 ml/8 fl oz) cream
3 teaspoons Dijon mustard
3 teaspoons drained and rinsed green peppercorns

TOPPING
400 g (13 oz) potatoes, quartered
1¹/₃ cups (165 g/5¹/₂ oz) self-raising flour
¹/₂ teaspoon salt
¹/₄ cup (30 g/1 oz) grated mature Cheddar
100 g (3¹/₂ oz) cold butter, chopped
1 egg yolk, lightly beaten, to glaze

1 Melt half the butter in a pan. When it begins to foam, add the chicken and cook until golden. Remove from the pan. Add the remaining butter and cook the leek and celery over medium heat until soft. Return the chicken to the pan.
2 Sprinkle the flour over the chicken and stir for about 1 minute. Remove from the heat and stir in the stock and cream. Mix well, making sure that there are no lumps. Return to the heat. Bring to the boil, then reduce the heat and simmer for about 20 minutes. Add the mustard and peppercorns and season to taste with salt and freshly ground black pepper. Transfer the mixture to a 1.25–1.5 litre capacity casserole dish and allow to cool. Preheat the oven to moderately hot 200°C (400°F/Gas 6).
3 To make the topping, cook the potato in a pan of boiling water until tender. Drain and mash until smooth. Place the flour and salt in a food processor and add the cheese and butter. Process in short bursts until the mixture forms crumbs. Add this mixture to the mashed potato and bring together with your hands to form a dough.
4 Roll out the dough on a floured surface, until it is 1 cm (¹/₂ inch) thick. Cut into circles with a 6 cm (2¹/₂ inch) diameter pastry cutter. Keep re-rolling the pastry scraps until all the dough is used. Carefully lift the circles up with your fingers, and arrange them so that they overlap on top of the cooled chicken and leek filling.
5 Brush the dough circles with the egg yolk and add a little milk if more glaze is needed. Bake for 30 minutes, or until the filling is heated through and the pastry is golden.

NUTRITION PER SERVE (6)
Protein 45 g; Fat 30 g; Carbohydrate 30 g; Dietary Fibre 4 g; Cholesterol 185 mg; 2405 kJ (570 Cal)

NOTE: For a lower-fat variation, you can use a non-stick frying pan to cook the chicken in Step 1. You can also replace the mature Cheddar with low-fat Cheddar and reduce the amount of butter used in the filling.

Rinse the leeks thoroughly before cooking, and slice very thinly.

Remove the pan from the heat and stir in the chicken stock and cream.

Add the mustard and peppercorns to the simmering chicken and leek mixture.

Bring together the crumb mixture and mashed potato with your hands.

Roll out the dough and cut circles from it with a pastry cutter.

Arrange the circles, overlapping, on top of the cooled filling mixture.

CHICKEN MEATLOAF

Preparation time: 15 minutes
Total cooking time: 1 hour 15 minutes
Serves 6

1 kg (2 lb) chicken mince
1 onion, grated
1 cup (90 g/3 oz) fresh white
    breadcrumbs (made from 2 slices
    of day-old bread)
2 eggs, lightly beaten
1/3 cup (80 ml) barbecue sauce

2 tablespoons Worcestershire sauce
1/4 cup (60 ml/2 fl oz) canned crushed
    tomatoes
2 tablespoons finely chopped fresh
    flat-leaf parsley

1 Preheat the oven to moderate
180°C (350°F/Gas 4). Mix together
the mince, onion, breadcrumbs,
egg, 2 tablespoons barbecue sauce,
Worcestershire sauce, crushed
tomatoes, parsley, salt and pepper.
2 Press into a lightly greased 1.5 litre
loaf tin. Place on an oven tray to catch

any spills and bake for 1 hour.
3 Pour off any fat from the tin. Spread
the remaining barbecue sauce over the
top of the meatloaf and bake for a
further 15 minutes. Turn out the
meatloaf and serve in slices.

NUTRITION PER SERVE
Protein 40 g; Fat 6 g; Carbohydrate 15 g;
Dietary Fibre 1 g; Cholesterol 145 mg;
1175 kJ (280 cal)

Mix together all the ingredients with your hands
until they are well combined.

Press the mixture into a lightly greased loaf tin
and bake for 1 hour.

Pour off any fat from the meatloaf and spread the
remaining barbecue sauce over the top.

TOMATO AND BACON QUICHE

Preparation time: 45 minutes + 1 hour
    refrigeration
Total cooking time: 1 hour 10 minutes
Serves 6

1¹/₂ cups (185 g/6 oz) plain flour
pinch of cayenne pepper
pinch of mustard powder
125 g (4 oz) butter, chilled and cubed
¹/₃ cup (40 g/1¹/₄ oz) grated Cheddar
1 egg yolk

FILLING
25 g (³/₄ oz) butter
100 g (3¹/₂ oz) lean bacon, chopped
1 small onion, finely sliced
3 eggs
³/₄ cup (185 ml/6 fl oz) cream
¹/₂ teaspoon salt
2 tomatoes, peeled, seeded and
    chopped into chunks
³/₄ cup (90 g/3 oz) grated Cheddar

1 Mix the flour, pepper, mustard and butter in a food processor until crumbly. Add the cheese and egg yolk and process in short bursts until the mixture comes together. Add 1–2 tablespoons of cold water if needed. Turn out onto a floured surface and gather into a ball. Wrap in plastic and refrigerate for 30 minutes. Grease a 23 cm (9 inch) loose-based deep tart tin.
2 To make the filling, melt the butter in a frying pan and cook the bacon for a few minutes until golden. Add the onion and cook until soft. Remove from the heat. Lightly beat the eggs, cream and salt together. Add the bacon and onion, then fold in the tomato and Cheddar.

3 Roll out the pastry on a floured surface until large enough to fit the tin. Trim the excess pastry and refrigerate for 30 minutes. Preheat the oven to 180°C (350°F/Gas 4). Cover the pastry with baking paper and spread with a layer of baking beads or rice. Bake for 10 minutes. Remove the paper and beads and bake for 10 minutes.
4 Pour the filling into the pastry shell and bake for 35 minutes until golden.

NUTRITION PER SERVE
Protein 15 g; Fat 45 g; Carbohydrate 25 g;
Dietary Fibre 2 g; Cholesterol 255 mg;
2405 kJ (570 cal)

Remove the rind and excess fat from the bacon and chop the meat.

Cook the bacon in a little butter until golden and then add the onion.

Fold the tomato chunks and Cheddar into the egg and cream mixture.

LEG OF LAMB

Preparation time: 15 minutes
Total cooking time: 1 hour 30 minutes
Serves 6

2 kg (4 lb) leg of lamb
4 cloves garlic, cut in
    half lengthways
6–8 sprigs fresh rosemary
2 tablespoons olive oil
2 tablespoons freshly
    ground black pepper

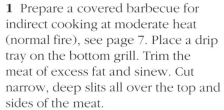

1 Prepare a covered barbecue for indirect cooking at moderate heat (normal fire), see page 7. Place a drip tray on the bottom grill. Trim the meat of excess fat and sinew. Cut narrow, deep slits all over the top and sides of the meat.
2 Push the halved garlic cloves and the rosemary sprigs into the cuts on the meat. Brush all over with oil and sprinkle with black pepper.
3 Put the lamb on the barbecue grill over the drip tray, cover and cook for 1 hour 30 minutes for medium-rare

meat. Brush with olive oil occasionally. Leave in a warm place, covered with foil, for 10–15 minutes before carving.

NUTRITION PER SERVE
Protein 41 g; Fat 10 g; Carbohydrate 0 g;
Dietary Fibre 0 g; Cholesterol 120 mg;
1085 kJ (260 cal)

Trim the lamb of excess fat and sinew before making small cuts all over it.

Push the halved cloves of garlic and the rosemary sprigs into the cuts.

Brush the lamb with olive oil occasionally while it is cooking.

BAKED VEGETABLES

Preparation time: 20 minutes
Total cooking time: 1 hour 15 minutes
Serves 6

6 potatoes
60 g (2 oz) butter, melted
1/4 teaspoon paprika
750 g (1 1/2 lb) pumpkin
6 small onions
150 g (5 oz) green beans, topped and
    tailed
150 g (5 oz) broccoli, cut into
    florets
30 g (1 oz) butter, chopped, extra

1 Prepare a covered barbecue for indirect cooking at moderate heat (normal fire), see page 7. Peel the potatoes and cut in half. Using a small, sharp knife, make deep, fine cuts in the potatoes, taking care not to cut all the way through. Take two large sheets of foil, fold in half and brush liberally with melted butter. Place the potatoes, unscored-side-down, on the foil and fold up the edges of the foil to create a tray. Brush the potatoes generously with melted butter and sprinkle with paprika.
2 Cut the pumpkin into 3 wedges and cut each wedge in half. Peel the onions and trim the bases slightly, so they will sit flat on the grill. Brush the

pumpkin and onions with melted butter. Place the pumpkin, onions and the tray of potatoes on the barbecue grill. Cover the barbecue and cook for 1 hour.
3 Put the beans and broccoli on a sheet of foil brushed with melted butter. Dot with the extra butter and wrap completely in the foil. Add to the other vegetables on the grill and cook for a further 15 minutes.

NUTRITION PER SERVE
Protein 8 g; Fat 4 g; Carbohydrate 26 g;
Dietary Fibre 6 g; Cholesterol 34 mg;
1020 kJ (240 cal)

Make deep fine cuts in the potatoes and then brush with butter and sprinkle with paprika.

Put the pumpkin, onions and tray of potatoes on the barbecue grill.

Put the beans and broccoli on a sheet of foil and dot with the extra butter.

CHICKEN AND BROCCOLI BAKE

Preparation time: 20 minutes
Total cooking time: 1 hour
Serves 6

30 g (1 oz) butter
4 chicken breast fillets, cut into cubes
6 spring onions, sliced
2 cloves garlic, crushed
2 tablespoons plain flour
1¹/₂ cups (375 ml/12 fl oz) chicken
    stock
2 teaspoons Dijon mustard
280 g (9 oz) broccoli, cut into florets
1 kg (2 lb) potatoes, cut into quarters
2 tablespoons milk
60 g (2 oz) butter, extra
2 eggs
¹/₃ cup (30 g/1 oz) flaked toasted
    almonds
snipped fresh chives, to garnish

1 Preheat the oven to moderate 180°C (350°F/Gas 4). Heat half the butter in a large frying pan, and cook the chicken in batches until browned and cooked through. Remove from the pan. In the same pan melt the remaining butter and cook the spring onion and garlic for 2 minutes. Stir in the flour and mix well. Pour in the stock and cook, stirring, until the mixture boils and thickens. Add the mustard and then stir in the chicken. Season well.
2 Meanwhile, steam or microwave the broccoli until just tender, taking care not to overcook it. Refresh the broccoli in iced water and drain well.
3 Boil the potato in plenty of salted water for 15–20 minutes, or until tender. Drain and mash well with the milk, extra butter and eggs. Put the broccoli in a 2.5 litre ovenproof dish

and pour in the chicken mixture. Pipe or spoon the mashed potato over the top. Sprinkle with the almonds and bake for 25 minutes, or until the top is browned and cooked through. Scatter the chives over the top before serving.

NUTRITION PER SERVE
Protein 25 g; Fat 20 g; Carbohydrate 25 g; Dietary Fibre 5.5 g; Cholesterol 135 mg; 1610 kJ (385 Cal)

Use a large sharp knife to cut the chicken breasts into cubes.

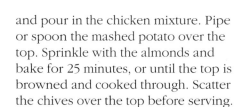

Add the chicken to the pan and cook in batches until browned.

Pour in the stock and stir over heat until the mixture thickens.

SEAFOOD QUICHE

Preparation time: 20 minutes +
  20 minutes refrigeration
Total cooking time: 1 hour
Serves 4–6

2 sheets shortcrust pastry

FILLING
30 g (1 oz) butter
300 g (10 oz) mixed raw seafood
    (prawns, scallops, crab meat)
3/4 cup (90 g/3 oz) grated Cheddar
3 eggs
1 tablespoon plain flour
1/4 teaspoon salt
1/2 teaspoon black pepper
1/2 cup (125 ml/4 fl oz) cream
1/2 cup (125 ml/4 fl oz) milk
1 small fennel, finely sliced
1 tablespoon grated Parmesan

1 Place the sheets of pastry slightly overlapping and roll out until large enough to fit a 23 cm (9 inch) loose-based tart tin. Trim away the excess pastry. Refrigerate for 20 minutes. Preheat the oven to 190°C (375°F/ Gas 5). Cover the pastry shell with baking paper and spread with a layer of baking beads or rice. Bake for 15 minutes. Remove the paper and beads and bake for 10 minutes, or until golden. Cool on a wire rack.
2 Heat the butter in a pan and cook the seafood for 2–3 minutes. Cool, then arrange in the pastry shell. Sprinkle with Cheddar.
3 Beat the eggs together and whisk in the flour, salt, pepper, cream and milk. Pour over the seafood filling. Sprinkle the fennel and Parmesan over the top.
4 Bake for 30–35 minutes. Leave to cool slightly before serving.

NUTRITION PER SERVE (6)
Protein 20 g; Fat 35 g; Carbohydrate 30 g;
Dietary Fibre 1 g; Cholesterol 220 mg;
2190 kJ (520 cal)

Fit the pastry into the flan tin, pressing it well into the sides.

Remove the baking paper and rice from the pastry shell.

Cook the seafood in the melted butter before putting into the pastry shell.

Sprinkle the Cheddar over the top of the seafood in the pastry shell.

HAM, CHEESE AND POTATO PIE

Preparation time: 25 minutes +
    cooling + 10 minutes standing
Total cooking time: 1 hour 45 minutes
Serves 6–8

1/4 cup (60 ml/2 fl oz) olive oil
3 onions, finely chopped
1 clove garlic, finely chopped
300 g (10 oz) ham, chopped
430 g (14 oz) desiree potatoes, diced
2 cups (250 g/8 oz) grated Cheddar
2 eggs
1/3 cup (80 ml/2³/4 fl oz) cream
2 teaspoons chopped fresh chives
4 sheets puff pastry
1 egg, lightly beaten, to glaze

1 Heat the oil in a large frying pan over medium heat. Add the onion and garlic and cook, stirring occasionally, for 5 minutes, or until the onion softens. Add the ham and potato and cook, stirring occasionally, for 5–7 minutes, or until the potato softens slightly. Transfer to a large bowl and stir in the Cheddar.

2 Mix together the eggs and cream and pour into the bowl. Add the chives and mix thoroughly. Season and leave to cool.

3 Preheat the oven to moderately hot 200°C (400°F/ Gas 6). Grease an 18 cm (7 inch) pie dish. Line the pie dish with two sheets of puff pastry, and brush the edge with beaten egg. Spoon the filling into the pie dish.

4 Cut the remaining sheets of pastry into quarters, and each quarter into three equal lengths. Place the strips, overlapping, around the top of the pie, leaving the centre open. Press down the edges so that the top and bottom layers stick together, then trim the edges with a sharp knife.

5 Brush the top of the pie with the beaten egg, and bake in the oven for 30 minutes. Reduce the temperature to 180°C (350°F/Gas 4) and cook the pie for another hour, covering the top with foil if it is browning too much. Leave for 10 minutes before serving.

NUTRITION PER SERVE (8)
Protein 24 g; Fat 44 g; Carbohydrate 39 g;
Dietary Fibre 3 g; Cholesterol 153 mg;
2700 kJ (645 Cal)

Pour the creamy egg mixture into the bowl with the ham and cheese.

Overlap the pastry strips around the pie, leaving a gap in the middle.

SPINACH PIE

Preparation time: 30 minutes +
  30 minutes chilling
Total cooking time: 1 hour
Serves 8–10

2 cups (250 g/8 oz) plain flour
1/3 cup (80 ml/2³/4 fl oz) olive oil
1 egg, beaten
4–5 tablespoons iced water

FILLING
1 kg (2 lb) spinach, stalks removed,
  roughly chopped
1 tablespoon olive oil
1 large leek, sliced
4 cloves garlic, crushed
2 cups (500 g/1 lb) ricotta
1 cup (90 g/3 oz) grated pecorino
  cheese
300 g (10 oz) feta, crumbled
3 eggs, lightly beaten
3 tablespoons chopped fresh dill
1/2 cup (15 g/1/2 oz) chopped fresh
  flat-leaf parsley

1 Sift the flour and 1/2 teaspoon salt
into a large bowl and make a well in
the centre. Mix the oil, egg and most
of the water, add to the flour and mix
with a flat-bladed knife until the
mixture comes together in beads,
adding a little more water if necessary.
Gather the dough and press into a ball.
Wrap in plastic wrap and chill for at
least 30 minutes.
2 Put the spinach in a large pan,
sprinkle lightly with water, then cover
and steam for 5 minutes until wilted.
Drain, squeeze out the excess
moisture, then finely chop.
3 Preheat the oven to 200°C (400°F/
Gas 6) and heat a baking tray. Grease
a 25 cm (12 inch) loose-based fluted
tart tin. Heat the oil in a frying pan and
cook the leek and garlic over low heat
for 5 minutes, or until soft. Mix with
the ricotta, pecorino, feta, spinach,
egg, dill and parsley and season with
salt and pepper.
4 Roll out two-thirds of the pastry
between two sheets of baking paper
until large enough to line the tin. Fill

with the spinach mixture. Roll out the
remaining pastry between the baking
paper and top the pie. Trim the edges
and make two or three steam holes.
5 Bake the pie on the hot tray for
15 minutes, then reduce the oven to
180°C (350°F/Gas 4) and cook for
another 30 minutes. Cover with foil if
the pie is overbrowning. Leave for
5–10 minutes before slicing.

NUTRITION PER SERVE (10)
Protein 20 g; Fat 26 g; Carbohydrate 20 g;
Dietary Fibre 4 g; Cholesterol 123 mg;
1660 kJ (395 cal)

Drain the wilted spinach well, then finely chop
with a large, sharp knife.

FAMILY CHICKEN PIE

Preparation time: 40 minutes
  + 20 minutes chilling
Total cooking time: 1 hour
Serves 6

PASTRY
2 cups (250 g/8 oz) self-raising flour
125 g (4 oz) butter, chopped
1 egg

FILLING
1 barbecued chicken
30 g (1 oz) butter
1 onion, finely chopped
310 g (10 oz) can creamed corn
1¼ cups (315 ml/10 fl oz) cream

1 To make the pastry, process the flour and butter in a food processor for 15 seconds, or until the mixture is fine and crumbly. Add the egg and 2–3 tablespoons water and process for 30 seconds, or until the mixture just comes together. Turn onto a lightly floured surface and gather together into a smooth ball. Cover with plastic wrap and refrigerate for 20 minutes.

2 Meanwhile, to make the filling, remove the meat from the chicken carcass and shred finely. Heat the butter in a pan and cook the onion over medium heat for 3 minutes. Add the chicken, corn and cream. Bring to the boil, then reduce the heat and simmer for 10 minutes. Remove from the heat and allow to cool slightly.

3 Preheat the oven to moderate 180°C (350°F/Gas 4). Roll half the pastry between two sheets of plastic wrap to cover the base and side of a 23 cm (9 inch) pie dish. Spoon the chicken mixture into the pastry-lined dish.

4 Roll the remaining pastry to cover the top of the pie. Brush with milk. Press the edges together to seal. Trim the edges with a sharp knife. Roll the excess pastry into two long ropes and twist together. Brush the pie edge with a little milk and place the pastry rope around the rim. Bake for 45 minutes.

NUTRITION PER SERVE
Protein 18 g; Fat 48 g; Carbohydrate 44 g;
Dietary Fibre 4 g; Cholesterol 212 mg;
2832 kJ (676 Cal)

Add the egg and water to the flour and butter mixture and process.

Add the chicken, corn and cream to the onion and bring to the boil.

Roll half the pastry out between two sheets of plastic wrap.

Brush the pie edge with a little milk, then place the pastry rope around the rim of the pie.

WELSH LAMB PIE

Preparation time: 20 minutes + cooling
Total cooking time: 2 hours 35 minutes
Serves 6

750 g (1 1/2 lb) boned lamb shoulder,
    cubed
3/4 cup (90 g/3 oz) plain flour,
    seasoned
2 tablespoons olive oil
200 g (6 1/2 oz) bacon, finely chopped
2 cloves garlic, chopped
4 large leeks, sliced
1 large carrot, chopped
2 large potatoes, diced
1 1/4 cups (315 ml/10 fl oz) beef stock
1 bay leaf
2 teaspoons chopped fresh parsley
375 g (12 oz) quick flaky pastry
1 egg, lightly beaten, to glaze

1 Toss the meat in the flour. Heat the oil in a large frying pan over medium heat and brown the meat in batches for 4–5 minutes, then remove from the pan. Cook the bacon in the pan for 3 minutes. Add the garlic and leek and cook for 5 minutes, or until soft.
2 Put the meat in a large saucepan, add the leek and bacon, carrot, potato, stock and bay leaf and bring to the boil, then reduce the heat, cover and simmer for 30 minutes. Uncover and simmer for 1 hour, or until the meat is cooked and the liquid has thickened. Season to taste. Remove the bay leaf, stir in the parsley and set aside to cool.
3 Preheat the oven to moderately 200°C (400°F/ Gas 6). Place the filling in an 18 cm (7 inch) pie dish. Roll out the pastry between two sheets of baking paper until large enough to cover the pie. Trim the edges and pinch to seal.
4 Decorate the pie with pastry trimmings. Cut two slits in the top for steam to escape. Brush with egg and bake for 45 minutes, or until the pastry is crisp and golden.

NUTRITION PER SERVE
Protein 42 g; Fat 28 g; Carbohydrate 43 g;
Dietary Fibre 5 g; Cholesterol 147 mg;
2465 kJ (590 Cal)

Cook the filling until the liquid has thickened and then remove the bay leaf.

Cut out shapes from the pastry trimmings to decorate the pie.

BAKED CHICKEN AND ARTICHOKE PANCAKES

Preparation time: 30 minutes
Total cooking time: 1 hour
Serves 4

1 teaspoon baking powder
1¹/₃ cups (165 g/5¹/₂ oz) plain flour
¹/₄ teaspoon salt
2 eggs
300 ml (10 fl oz) milk
90 g (3 oz) butter
2¹/₂ cups (600 ml/20 fl oz) chicken
  stock
2 egg yolks
1 cup (250 ml/8 fl oz) cream
1 teaspoon lemon juice
300 g (10 oz) cooked chicken,
  chopped roughly
350 g (11 oz) artichoke hearts, drained
  and sliced
2 teaspoons chopped fresh thyme
2 teaspoons chopped fresh parsley
100 g (3¹/₂ oz) grated Parmesan

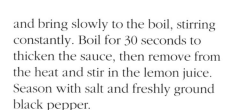

1 Sift the baking powder, 1 cup (125 g/4 oz) flour and salt into a large bowl and make a well in the centre. Whisk the eggs and milk in a jug and pour into the well, whisking until just smooth. Heat a frying pan and brush lightly with melted butter. Add ¹/₄ cup (60 ml/2 fl oz) batter and cook over medium heat until the underside is brown. Turn over and cook the other side. Transfer to a plate and cover with a tea towel while cooking the remaining batter.

2 Melt the butter in a pan and stir in the remaining flour. Cook for 2 minutes, then remove from the heat. Slowly whisk in the chicken stock until smooth. Whisk in the combined egg yolks and cream. Return to the heat and bring slowly to the boil, stirring constantly. Boil for 30 seconds to thicken the sauce, then remove from the heat and stir in the lemon juice. Season with salt and freshly ground black pepper.

3 Preheat the oven to moderately hot 200°C (400°F/Gas 6). Grease a 3 litre ovenproof dish with melted butter. Line the base with 2 pancakes, slightly overlapping. Spoon half of the chicken, artichokes and herbs evenly over the pancakes. Pour a third of the sauce over the top and layer with another two pancakes. Repeat, finishing with a layer of 3 pancakes. Spread the remaining sauce over the top, sprinkle with the Parmesan and bake for 30–35 minutes, or until golden brown.

NUTRITION PER SERVE
Protein 40 g; Fat 60 g; Carbohydrate 37 g; Dietary Fibre 4 g; Cholesterol 305 mg; 3568 kJ (850 Cal)

Heat a frying pan, add the batter and cook until the underside is brown.

Slowly whisk in the combined yolks and cream, away from the heat.

Line the dish with pancakes, then spoon in half the chicken and artichoke filling.

SHEPHERD'S PIE

Preparation time: 30 minutes
Total cooking time: 1 hour 20 minutes
Serves 6

1 kg (2 lb) potatoes
30 g (1 oz) butter
2 tablespoons milk
1 tablespoon oil
1 large onion, finely chopped
1 kg (2 lb) lamb mince
1 carrot, finely chopped
2 tablespoons plain flour
1 cup (250 ml/8 fl oz) vegetable stock
2 tablespoons Worcestershire sauce
1 cup (155 g/5 oz) frozen peas

1 Peel the potatoes and cut into chunks. Cook in a large pan of boiling water for 15–20 minutes, or until tender. Drain the potato well and return to the pan over low heat, and stir to evaporate any excess water. Remove from the heat, add the butter and milk, and mash with a potato masher until smooth. Season with salt and cracked pepper. Preheat the oven to moderate 180°C (350°F/Gas 4).

2 Meanwhile, heat the oil in a large frying pan and add the onion. Cook, stirring occasionally, until soft and just beginning to colour. Add the mince, increase the heat and cook until browned, breaking up any lumps with a wooden spoon as the meat cooks.

3 Add the carrot to the pan and cook for a few minutes until just tender.

Sprinkle on the flour and cook, stirring, for 1 minute. Slowly add the stock, stirring constantly. Add the Worcestershire sauce. Bring to the boil and cook for 2–3 minutes, or until the gravy thickens. Season to taste with salt and pepper. Stir in the peas and transfer the mixture to a 2 litre ovenproof dish.

4 Spoon the mashed potato onto the meat mixture and spread out evenly. Use a fork to swirl the surface. Bake for 40–50 minutes, or until the potato is golden.

NUTRITION PER SERVE
Protein 40 g; Fat 20 g; Carbohydrate 30 g; Dietary Fibre 5 g; Cholesterol 105 mg; 1995 kJ (475 Cal)

Cook the mince until browned, breaking up any lumps as you go.

Sprinkle the flour over the mince mixture and stir to blend it in.

Use a fork to swirl the surface of the mashed potato.

ROSEMARY LAMB COBBLER

Preparation time: 30 minutes
Total cooking time: 2 hours
Serves 4–6

600 g (1¼ lb) boned lamb leg, cut into small chunks
¼ cup (30 g/1 oz) plain flour, seasoned
30 g (1 oz) butter
2 tablespoons olive oil
8 spring onions, chopped
3 cloves garlic, crushed
2 cups (500 ml/16 fl oz) beef stock
1 cup (250 ml/8 fl oz) dry white wine
2 teaspoons wholegrain mustard
2 teaspoons finely chopped fresh rosemary
2 celery sticks, sliced
1 teaspoon grated lemon rind
1 teaspoon lemon juice
½ cup (125 g/4 oz) sour cream

COBBLER TOPPING
¾ cup (185 ml/6 fl oz) milk
1 egg
2 tablespoons melted butter
1½ cups (185 g/6 oz) plain flour
2 teaspoons baking powder
1 teaspoon finely chopped fresh rosemary
2 tablespoons finely chopped fresh flat-leaf parsley

1 Put the lamb pieces and flour in a plastic bag and shake well to evenly coat the lamb. Shake off any excess.
2 Heat the butter and 1 tablespoon of the olive oil in a large saucepan over high heat, then cook half the lamb for 5 minutes, or until well browned. Add the remaining oil if needed and cook the remaining lamb.

3 Add half the spring onion to the pan with the garlic and cook for 30 seconds, or until the spring onion is softened. Return all the lamb to the pan with the stock, wine, mustard, rosemary, celery, lemon rind and juice and bring to the boil. Reduce the heat and simmer, stirring occasionally, for 1¼ hours, or until the lamb is tender and the sauce has thickened.
4 Remove from the heat and stir a little of the sauce into the sour cream, then stir it all back into the lamb mixture with the remaining spring onion. Leave to cool while you make the topping.
5 Preheat the oven to moderately hot 190°C (375°F/ Gas 5). To make the topping, combine the milk, egg and melted butter in a large bowl. Add the combined sifted flour and baking powder with the herbs, 1 teaspoon salt and some cracked black pepper and stir until you have a thick, sticky batter—you may need to add a little more flour if it is too wet, or milk if it is too dry.
6 Spoon the lamb into a deep 18 cm (7 inch) pie dish and, using two spoons, cover the top with small dollops of the batter, leaving a little space for spreading. Cook for 30 minutes, or until the topping is risen and golden.

NUTRITION PER SERVE (6)
Protein 31 g; Fat 28 g; Carbohydrate 31 g; Dietary Fibre 2.5 g; Cholesterol 153 mg; 2180 kJ (520 Cal)

Put the lamb and flour in a plastic bag and shake until the meat is lightly covered.

Cook the lamb in two batches in a large saucepan until it is nicely browned.

Simmer the mixture until the meat is tender and the sauce has thickened.

Stir a little of the meaty sauce into the sour cream.

Stir the batter for the cobbler topping until it is thick and sticky.

Add spoonfuls of the batter to the top of the pie, leaving a little room for spreading.

desserts

LEMON DELICIOUS

Preparation time: 10 minutes
Total cooking time: 40 minutes
Serves 4

30 g (1 oz) butter, softened
3/4 cup (185 g/6 oz) caster sugar
1 teaspoon grated lemon rind
3 eggs, separated
1/4 cup (30 g/1 oz) plain flour
1/2 cup (125 ml/4 fl oz) lemon juice
1 1/2 cups (375 ml/12 fl oz) warm milk
icing sugar, to dust

1 Preheat the oven to moderate 180°C (350°F/Gas 4). Brush a 1.5 litre heatproof dish with melted butter. Place the butter, sugar, lemon rind and egg yolks in a bowl. Using electric beaters, beat until light and creamy.
2 Fold in the sifted flour in two batches, alternately with the lemon juice and milk. In a separate clean dry bowl, using electric beaters, whisk the egg whites until soft peaks form. Pour the lemon mixture down the inside of the bowl of beaten egg whites and fold the whites gently into the mixture.

3 Pour the combined mixture into the prepared dish and put the dish in a baking tin. Pour in enough warm water to come halfway up the side of the dish. Bake for 40 minutes, or until puffed and golden. Dust with icing sugar and serve with ice cream.

NUTRITION PER SERVE
Protein 9 g; Fat 15 g; Carbohydrate 60 g;
Dietary Fibre 0 g; Cholesterol 165 mg;
1630 kJ (390 Cal)

VARIATION: Try using limes or oranges for a new flavour.

Fold in the flour alternately with the lemon juice and milk.

Pour the lemon mixture down the inside of the bowl of beaten egg whites.

Gently fold the egg whites into the mixture with a spoon.

APPLE PIE

Preparation time: 45 minutes +
  cooling time
Total cooking time: 50 minutes
Serves 6

FILLING
6 large Granny Smith apples
2 tablespoons caster sugar
1 teaspoon finely grated lemon rind
pinch ground cloves

PASTRY
2 cups (250 g/8 oz) plain flour
3 tablespoons self-raising flour
150 g (5 oz) cold butter, chopped
2 tablespoons caster sugar
4–5 tablespoons iced water
2 tablespoons apricot jam
1 egg, lightly beaten
1 tablespoon sugar

1 Peel, core and cut the apples into wedges. Place in a heavy-based pan with the sugar, lemon rind, cloves and 2 tablespoons water. Cover and cook gently for 8 minutes, or until the apple is just tender, shaking the pan occasionally. Drain and allow to cool completely.

2 Sift the flours into a bowl and add the butter. Rub the butter into the flour using your fingertips until it resembles fine breadcrumbs. Add the sugar, mix well, and then make a well in the centre. Add the water and mix with a flat-bladed knife, using a cutting action, until the mixture comes together in beads. Gather the pastry together on a floured surface. Divide into two, making one half a little bigger. Cover with plastic wrap and refrigerate for 20 minutes.

3 Preheat the oven to moderately hot 200°C (400°F/Gas 6). Roll out the larger piece of pastry between two sheets of baking paper to line the base and side of a 23 cm (9 inch) pie plate. Peel off the top piece of paper and invert the pastry into the dish. Peel off the other baking sheet and trim off the excess pastry. Brush the jam over the base and spoon the apple filling into the shell. Roll out the remaining piece of pastry between the baking paper until large enough to cover the pie. Brush a little water around the rim, then place the top on, inverting the pastry off the baking paper. Trim off the excess pastry, pinch the edges together and cut a couple of steam slits in the top.

4 Bring together the excess pastry bits, gently re-roll and cut into leaves to decorate the top. Brush the top lightly with egg then sprinkle on the sugar. Bake for 20 minutes, then reduce the temperature to moderate 180°C (350°F/Gas 4) and bake for a further 15–20 minutes, or until golden.

NUTRITION PER SERVE
Protein 6.5 g; Fat 20 g; Carbohydrate 60 g; Dietary Fibre 3.5 g; Cholesterol 95 mg; 1955 kJ (465 Cal)

Roll out the pastry between two sheets of baking paper.

Invert the pastry into the pie dish and peel off the baking paper.

Put the pastry lid on the pie and trim off any excess pastry.

RICE PUDDING

Preparation time: 10 minutes
Total cooking time: 2 hours
Serves 4

¼ cup (55 g/2 oz) short-grain rice
1²/₃ cups (410 ml/13 fl oz) milk
1½ tablespoons caster sugar
¾ cup (185 ml/6 fl oz) cream
¼ teaspoon vanilla essence
¼ teaspoon grated nutmeg
1 bay leaf

1 Preheat the oven to slow 150°C (300°F/Gas 2) and grease a 1 litre ovenproof dish. In a bowl, mix together the rice, milk, caster sugar, cream and vanilla essence, and pour into the greased dish. Dust the surface with the grated nutmeg and float the bay leaf on top.

2 Bake the rice pudding for 2 hours, by which time the rice should have absorbed most of the milk and will have become creamy in texture with a brown skin on top. Serve hot.

NUTRITION PER SERVE
Protein 5 g; Fat 24 g; Carbohydrate 25 g; Dietary Fibre 0 g; Cholesterol 77 mg; 1378 kJ (330 Cal)

VARIATION: Add grated lemon or orange rind to give a citrus flavour.

Mix together the rice, milk, caster sugar, cream and vanilla essence.

Pour the mixture into a greased ovenproof dish and dust with nutmeg.

Float the bay leaf on the top to allow its flavours to infuse.

GRANDMOTHER'S PAVLOVA

Preparation time: 30 minutes
Total cooking time: 1 hour
Serves 6

4 egg whites
1 cup (250 g/8 oz) caster sugar
2 teaspoons cornflour
1 teaspoon white vinegar
2 cups (500 ml/16 fl oz) cream
3 passionfruit
strawberries, for decoration

1 Preheat the oven to warm 160°C (315°F/Gas 2–3). Line a 32 x 28 cm (13 x 11 inch) baking tray with a sheet of baking paper.
2 Place the egg whites and a pinch of salt in a small, dry bowl. Using electric beaters, beat until stiff peaks form. Add the sugar gradually, beating after each addition, until thick and glossy and all the sugar has dissolved.
3 Using a metal spoon, fold in the cornflour and vinegar. Spoon the mixture into a mound on the prepared tray. Flatten the top and smooth the sides. (The pavlova should be about 2.5 cm/1 inch high.) Bake for 1 hour, or until pale cream and crisp. Remove from the oven while warm and carefully turn upside down onto a plate. Allow to cool.
4 Lightly whip the cream until soft peaks form and spread over the soft centre. Decorate with pulp from the passionfruit and halved strawberries. Cut into wedges to serve.

NUTRITION PER SERVE
Protein 4 g; Fat 36 g; Carbohydrate 45 g;
Dietary Fibre 1.5 g; Cholesterol 113 mg;
2124 kJ (507 Cal)

Beat until the mixture is thick and glossy and all the sugar has dissolved.

Spoon the mixture onto the baking tray with a metal spoon.

Smooth the top and sides to give the pavlova a cake shape.

CREAMY CHOCOLATE MOUSSE

Preparation time: 5 minutes +
  overnight chilling
Total cooking time: 5 minutes
Serves 6

125 g (4 oz) dark chocolate, chopped
4 eggs, separated
¾ cup (185 ml/6 fl oz) cream, lightly
  whipped

1 Put the chocolate in a heatproof bowl. Bring a pan of water to a simmer, remove from the heat and place the bowl over the pan (don't let the base of the bowl touch the water). Stir the chocolate occasionally until melted. Remove from the heat and cool slightly. Lightly beat the egg yolks and stir into the chocolate mixture. Fold in the cream.

2 Using electric beaters, whisk the egg whites in a small dry bowl until soft peaks form. Fold one spoonful of the egg whites into the mousse with a metal spoon, then gently fold in the remainder, quickly and lightly.

3 Pour the mousse into six wine glasses or ¾ cup (185 ml/6 fl oz) ramekins. Cover with plastic wrap and refrigerate for 4 hours or overnight. Top with extra whipped cream and dust with cocoa powder, if desired.

NUTRITION PER SERVE
Protein 6 g; Fat 22 g; Carbohydrate 15 g;
Dietary Fibre 0 g; Cholesterol 160 mg;
1150 kJ (275 Cal)

Put the bowl of chocolate over a pan of simmering water and stir occasionally.

Gently fold the egg whites into the mousse with a metal spoon.

Pour the mousse into wine glasses or ramekins before covering and chilling.

PECAN PIE

Preparation time: 30 minutes + chilling
Total cooking time: 1 hour 15 minutes
Serves 6

1½ cups (185 g/6 oz) plain flour
100 g (3½ oz) cold butter, chopped
2 tablespoons iced water

FILLING
2 cups (200 g/6½ oz) whole pecans
3 eggs
60 g (2 oz) butter, melted
2/3 cup (155 g/5 oz) soft brown sugar
2/3 cup (170 ml/5½ fl oz) corn syrup
1 teaspoon vanilla essence

1 Sift the flour into a bowl and rub in the butter with your fingertips until the mixture resembles fine breadcrumbs. Add the water and mix it in with a flat-bladed knife, using a cutting action, until the mixture comes together in beads. Gather the dough together, cover with plastic wrap and refrigerate for 20 minutes.
2 Transfer the dough to a sheet of baking paper and roll it out to a 3 mm (1/8 inch) thickness. It should be large enough to line a 23 cm (9 inch) pie dish, with some pastry left over to decorate the edge. Invert the pastry into the dish and remove the baking paper. Line the dish with the pastry, and remove the excess. Gather the dough scraps together and roll them out to a 3 mm (1/8 inch) thickness. Using small cutters, cut shapes from the pastry (if you are making leaves, score veins into the leaves with a small sharp knife). Brush the pastry rim with water, and attach the pastry shapes. Chill for 20 minutes. Preheat the oven to moderate 180°C (350°F/Gas 4).

3 Cover the decorative edge of the pastry with wide strips of foil to prevent burning. Line the pastry shell with a sheet of crumpled greaseproof paper and fill with baking beads or rice. Bake for 15 minutes, then remove the beads and paper and bake for 15 minutes more, until the base is lightly golden and dry. Remove the foil and set aside to cool before filling.
4 Place the pecans on the pastry base. Whisk together the eggs, butter, sugar, syrup, vanilla and a good pinch of salt.

Pour over the pecans. Place the pie dish on a baking tray, and bake for 45 minutes. Cool completely.

NUTRITION PER SERVE
Protein 10 g; Fat 50 g; Carbohydrate 50 g; Dietary Fibre 4 g; Cholesterol 160 mg; 2780 kJ (665 Cal)

NOTE: Use any decorative shape you like for the edge. Simple leaf shapes can be cut free-hand from the pastry, if you do not have small cutters.

Invert the pastry into the pie dish, then remove the baking paper.

Use small cutters to make pastry shapes to decorate the pie edge.

Arrange the pecans evenly over the cooled pastry base.

GOLDEN SYRUP DUMPLINGS

Preparation time: 15 minutes
Total cooking time: 30 minutes
Serves 4

1 cup (125 g/4 oz) self-raising flour
40 g (1¼ oz) cold butter, chopped
1 egg
1 tablespoon milk
1 cup (250 g/8 oz) sugar
40 g butter, extra
2 tablespoons golden syrup
¼ cup (60 ml/2 fl oz) lemon juice

1 Sift the flour into a bowl and add a pinch of salt. Using your fingertips, rub the butter into the flour until the mixture resembles fine breadcrumbs, and make a well in the centre. Using a flat-bladed knife, stir the combined egg and milk into the flour mixture to form a soft dough.
2 To make the syrup, place 2 cups (500 ml/16 fl oz) water in a large pan with the sugar, butter, golden syrup and lemon juice. Stir over medium heat until combined and the sugar has dissolved.
3 Bring to the boil, then gently drop dessertspoons of the dough into the syrup. Reduce the heat to a simmer and cook, covered, for 20 minutes, or until a knife inserted into a dumpling comes out clean. Spoon onto serving plates, drizzle with syrup, and serve immediately with whipped cream.

NUTRITION PER SERVE
Protein 5 g; Fat 20 g; Carbohydrate 95 g;
Dietary Fibre 1 g; Cholesterol 97 mg;
2327 kJ (555 Cal)

Rub the butter into the flour until the mixture resembles breadcrumbs.

Stir the milk and egg into the flour mixture with a flat-bladed knife.

Carefully drop dessertspoons of dough into the boiling syrup.

BREAD AND BUTTER PUDDING

Preparation time: 15 minutes +
  45 minutes standing
Total cooking time: 40 minutes
Serves 4

30 g (1 oz) butter
8 thick slices day-old bread
2 tablespoons sultanas
3 tablespoons caster sugar
1 teaspoon mixed spice

3 eggs, beaten
2 teaspoons vanilla essence
700 ml (23 fl oz) milk
1/2 cup (125 ml/4 fl oz) cream
1 tablespoon demerara sugar

1 Lightly grease a 22 x 18 x 8 cm
(9 x 7 x 3 inch) ceramic ovenproof
dish. Butter the bread and cut each
slice in half on the diagonal. Layer
the bread into the prepared dish,
and sprinkle the combined sultanas,
caster sugar and mixed spice over
the top.

2 Whisk the eggs, vanilla, milk
and cream and pour over the bread.
Leave to stand for 45 minutes, then top
with the demerara sugar. Preheat the
oven to moderate 180°C (350°F/Gas 4).
3 Bake for about 35–40 minutes, or
until the custard around the bread has
set—check the very centre of the dish.
Serve hot.

NUTRITION PER SERVE
Protein 15 g; Fat 30 g; Carbohydrate 50 g;
Dietary Fibre 1.5 g; Cholesterol 220 mg;
2300 kJ (550 Cal)

Cut the bread slices in half diagonally and layer
them in the prepared dish.

Slowly pour the combined eggs, vanilla, milk and
cream over the bread.

Leave to soak, then scatter the demerara sugar
over the top.

BAKED CHEESECAKE

Preparation time: 30 minutes +
  20 minutes refrigeration + chilling
Total cooking time: 55 minutes
Serves 8

250 g (8 oz) butternut cookies
1 teaspoon mixed spice
100 g (3$^1/2$ oz) butter, melted
500 g (1 lb) cream cheese,
   softened
$^2/3$ cup (160 g/5$^1/2$ oz) caster sugar
4 eggs
1 teaspoon vanilla essence
1 tablespoon orange juice
1 tablespoon finely grated orange
   rind

TOPPING
1 cup (250 g/8 oz) sour cream
$^1/2$ teaspoon vanilla essence
3 teaspoons orange juice
1 tablespoon caster sugar
freshly grated nutmeg

1 Lightly grease the base of a 20 cm (8 inch) springform tin. Finely crush the biscuits in a food processor for 30 seconds, or put them in a plastic bag and roll with a rolling pin. Transfer to a bowl and add the mixed spice and butter. Stir until all the crumbs are moistened, then spoon into the tin and press firmly into the base and side. Chill for 20 minutes, or until firm.

2 Preheat the oven to 180°C (350°F/ Gas 4). Beat the cream cheese until smooth. Add the sugar and beat until smooth. Add the eggs, one at a time, beating well after each addition. Mix in the vanilla, orange juice and rind.

3 Pour the mixture into the crumb case and bake for 45 minutes, or until just firm. To make the topping, combine the sour cream, vanilla, orange juice and sugar in a bowl. Spread over the hot cheesecake, sprinkle with nutmeg and return to the oven for 7 minutes. Cool, then refrigerate until firm.

NUTRITION PER SERVE
Protein 10 g; Fat 50 g; Carbohydrate 45 g; Dietary Fibre 0.5 g; Cholesterol 230 mg; 2885 kJ (690 cal)

Press the biscuit mixture into a springform tin with the back of a spoon.

Add the eggs one at a time to the cream cheese mixture and beat well.

When the filling is smooth, mix in the vanilla, orange juice and rind.

PLUM COBBLER

Preparation time: 25 minutes
Total cooking time: 35 minutes
Serves 6

750 g (1½ lb) plums
⅓ cup (90 g/3 oz) sugar
1 teaspoon vanilla essence

TOPPING
1 cup (125 g/4 oz) self-raising
    flour
60 g (2 oz) cold butter, chopped
¼ cup (55 g/2 oz) firmly packed
    soft brown sugar
¼ cup (60 ml/2 fl oz) milk
1 tablespoon caster sugar

1 Preheat the oven to moderately hot 200°C (400°F/Gas 6). Cut the plums into quarters and remove the stones. Put the plums, sugar and 2 tablespoons water into a pan and bring to the boil, stirring, until the sugar dissolves.
2 Reduce the heat, then cover and simmer for 5 minutes, or until the plums are tender. Remove the skins from the plums if desired. Add the vanilla essence and spoon the mixture into a 3 cup (750 ml/24 fl oz) ovenproof dish.
3 To make the topping, sift the flour into a large bowl and add the butter. Using your fingertips, rub the butter into the flour until it resembles fine breadcrumbs. Stir in the brown sugar and 2 tablespoons milk.

4 Stir with a knife to form a soft dough, adding more milk if necessary. Turn the mixture out onto a lightly floured surface and gather together to form a smooth dough. Roll out until the dough is 1 cm (½ inch) thick and cut into rounds using a 4 cm (1½ inch) cutter.
5 Overlap the rounds around the side of the dish over the filling. (The plums in the middle will not be covered.) Lightly brush with milk and sprinkle with sugar. Cook in the oven on a baking tray for 30 minutes, or until the topping is golden and cooked through.

NUTRITION PER SERVE
Protein 3 g; Fat 9 g; Carbohydrate 50 g;
Dietary Fibre 3.5 g; Cholesterol 25 mg;
1245 kJ (295 Cal)

Sift the flour into a bowl, then rub in the butter with your fingertips.

Stir with a flat-bladed knife to form a soft dough, adding more milk if necessary.

Roll out the dough to a thickness of 1 cm (½ inch), then cut into rounds.

BANANA FRITTERS

Preparation time: 20 minutes +
 30 minutes standing
Total cooking time: 10 minutes
Serves 4

1 cup (125 g/4 oz) self-raising flour
1 tablespoon caster sugar
1 teaspoon ground cinnamon
oil, for deep-frying
4 bananas

1 Sift the flour and a pinch of salt into a bowl. Make a well in the centre, and gradually add 1 cup (250 ml/8 fl oz) water while gently whisking, drawing the flour in from the sides. Whisk until just combined. The batter will be slightly lumpy—overbeating the batter will make it tough. Stand for 30 minutes. Combine the sugar and cinnamon in a bowl, and set aside.
2 Fill a large deep pan one-third full of oil. Heat to 180°C (350°F), or until a cube of bread dropped into the oil browns in 15 seconds.
3 Cut the bananas in half crossways, slightly on the diagonal. Dip them into the batter. Quickly drain off any excess batter and deep-fry in the hot oil for 2 minutes, or until crisp and golden. The best way to do this is to use two pairs of tongs —one to dip the bananas in the batter and lift into the oil, and one to remove from the oil. Drain on crumpled paper towels. Repeat with the remaining bananas. Sprinkle with the cinnamon sugar and serve with ice cream or cream.

NUTRITION PER SERVE
Protein 3.5 g; Fat 15 g; Carbohydrate 35 g;
Dietary Fibre 2 g; Cholesterol 0 mg;
1153 kJ (275 Cal)

Whisk the flour and water until the batter is just combined.

Heat the oil until a cube of bread dropped into the oil browns in 15 seconds.

Deep-fry the bananas until the batter is crisp and golden.

STICKY DATE PUDDING

Preparation time: 25 minutes +
    15 minutes standing
Total cooking time: 50 minutes
Serves 8

1 cup (185 g/6 oz) pitted dates
1 teaspoon bicarbonate of soda
90 g (3 oz) butter, softened
1/2 cup (115 g/4 oz) firmly packed soft
    brown sugar
2 eggs, lightly beaten
1 teaspoon vanilla essence
11/2 cups (185 g/6 oz) self-raising flour

SAUCE
1 cup (230 g/71/2 oz) firmly packed
    soft brown sugar

1 cup (250 ml/8 fl oz) cream
90 g (3 oz) butter
1/2 teaspoon vanilla essence

1 Preheat the oven to moderate 180°C
(350°F/Gas 4). Brush a deep 18 cm
(7 inch) square cake tin with melted
butter and line the base with baking
paper. Put the chopped dates and
soda in a heatproof bowl and add
1 cup (250 ml/8 fl oz) boiling water.
Stir and leave for 15 minutes.
2 Using electric beaters, beat the
butter and brown sugar until light
and creamy. Beat in the eggs gradually.
Add the vanilla essence. Fold in half
of the sifted flour then half of the date
mixture. Stir in the remaining flour
and dates, mixing well. Pour into the
prepared tin and cook for 50 minutes,

or until cooked when tested with a
skewer. Leave the pudding in the tin
to cool for 10 minutes before turning
out. Serve warm with the hot sauce.
3 To make the sauce, put the sugar,
cream, butter and vanilla in a pan and
bring to the boil while stirring. Reduce
the heat and simmer for 5 minutes.

NUTRITION PER SERVE
Protein 5 g; Fat 33 g; Carbohydrate 75 g;
Dietary Fibre 3 g; Cholesterol 145 mg;
2530 kJ (605 Cal)

Using a sharp knife, chop the dates into small
pieces.

Pour boiling water over the dates and bicarbonate
of soda.

Put the brown sugar, cream, butter and vanilla
essence in a pan and simmer.

LEMON MERINGUE PIE

Preparation time: 1 hour + chilling
Total cooking time: 45 minutes
Serves 6

1½ cups (185 g/6 oz) plain flour
2 tablespoons icing sugar
125 g (4 oz) cold butter, chopped
2–3 tablespoons iced water

FILLING
¼ cup (30 g/1 oz) cornflour
¼ cup (30 g/1 oz) plain flour
1 cup (250 g/8 oz) caster sugar
¾ cup (185 ml/6 fl oz) lemon juice
3 teaspoons grated lemon rind
40 g (1¼ oz) butter
6 eggs, separated
1½ cups (375 g/12 oz) caster sugar,
    extra
½ teaspoon cornflour, extra

1 Sift the flour into a bowl and add the icing sugar and butter. Using your fingertips, rub in the butter until the mixture resembles breadcrumbs. Add 2 tablespoons water and mix into the flour with a flat-bladed knife using a cutting action until the mixture comes together in small beads, then gather the dough together. Add the remaining water if the dough is too dry.
2 Transfer the dough to a sheet of baking paper and roll out until large enough to line a greased 23 cm (9 inch) round pie plate. Ease the pastry into the prepared dish. Trim off any excess pastry and pinch or fork the edge to decorate. Refrigerate for 15 minutes.
3 Preheat the oven to moderate 180°C (350°F/Gas 4). Place a sheet of baking paper in the pie shell and spread a layer of baking beads or rice over the top. Bake for 10–15 minutes, then

remove the paper and beads, and bake for a further 10 minutes, or until the pastry is cooked through. Remove from the oven and cool completely.
4 To make the filling, place the flours and sugar in a pan. Whisk in the lemon juice, rind and 1½ cups (375 ml/12 fl oz) water. Whisk constantly over medium heat until the mixture boils and thickens, then reduce the heat and cook for 1 minute. Remove from the heat then whisk in the butter and egg yolks, one at a time. Cover the surface with plastic wrap and cool.
5 Preheat the oven to hot 220°C (425°F/Gas 7). Spread the filling into

the pastry shell. Place the egg whites and extra sugar in a mixing bowl. Beat with electric beaters on high for 10 minutes, or until the sugar is almost completely dissolved and the meringue is thick and glossy. Beat in the extra cornflour. Spread the meringue over the top of the pie, piling it high towards the centre. Bake for 5–10 minutes, or until lightly browned. Cool before serving.

NUTRITION PER SERVE
Protein 4 g; Fat 18 g; Carbohydrate 80 g; Dietary Fibre 1.5 g; Cholesterol 53 mg; 2020 kJ (483 Cal)

Remove the paper, beans or rice and bake until the pastry is cooked through.

Whisk the lemon mixture over medium heat until it boils and thickens.

Beat the egg whites and sugar until the meringue is thick and glossy.

PUMPKIN PIE

Preparation time: 20 minutes +
  40 minutes refrigeration + cooling
Total cooking time: 1 hour 30 minutes
Serves 6–8

1¼ cups (150 g/5 oz) plain flour
100 g (3½ oz) unsalted butter, chilled
    and cubed
2 teaspoons caster sugar
4 tablespoons iced water

FILLING
750 g (1½ lb) butternut pumpkin,
    cubed
2 eggs, lightly beaten
1 cup (185 g/6 oz) soft brown sugar
⅓ cup (80 ml/2¾ fl oz) cream
1 tablespoon sweet sherry or brandy
½ teaspoon ground ginger
½ teaspoon ground nutmeg
1 teaspoon ground cinnamon

1 Sift the flour into a large bowl and rub in the butter with your fingertips until the mixture resembles fine breadcrumbs. Mix in the caster sugar. Make a well in the centre, add almost all the water and mix with a flat-bladed knife, using a cutting action, until the mixture comes together in beads, adding more water if needed.
2 Gather the dough together and lift out onto a lightly floured work surface. Press into a disc. Wrap in plastic and refrigerate for 20 minutes.
3 Roll out the pastry between two sheets of baking paper until large enough to line an 18 cm (7 inch) pie dish. Line the dish with pastry, trim away the excess and crimp the edges with a fork. Cover with plastic wrap and refrigerate for 20 minutes.
4 Preheat the oven to 180°C (350°F/Gas 4). Cook the pumpkin in boiling water until tender. Drain, mash, push through a sieve and leave to cool.
5 Line the pastry shell with baking paper and spread with a layer of baking beads or rice. Bake for 10 minutes, then remove the paper and beads and bake for 10 minutes, or until lightly golden. Set aside to cool.
6 Whisk the eggs and sugar together in a large bowl. Add the cooled pumpkin, cream, sherry and the spices and stir thoroughly. Pour into the pastry shell, smooth the surface and bake for 1 hour, or until set. If the pastry overbrowns, cover the edges with foil. Cool before serving.

NUTRITION PER SERVE (8)
Protein 6 g; Fat 16.5 g; Carbohydrate
45 g; Dietary Fibre 2 g; Cholesterol
90 mg; 1470 kJ (350 cal)

Bake the pastry for 10 minutes, then remove the paper and beads and cook until golden.

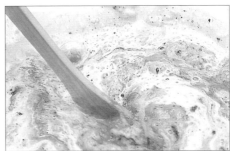

Stir the pumpkin, cream, sherry and spices into the egg and sugar mixture.

SELF-SAUCING CHOCOLATE PUDDING

Preparation time: 10 minutes
Total cooking time: 40 minutes
Serves 6

1 cup (125 g/4 oz) self-raising flour
3 tablespoons cocoa powder
1/2 cup (125 g/4 oz) caster sugar
1 egg
1/2 cup (125 ml/4 fl oz) milk
60 g (2 oz) butter, melted
1 teaspoon vanilla essence
1 cup (185 g/6 oz) soft brown sugar

1 Preheat the oven to moderate 180°C (350°F/Gas 4). Brush a 2 litre heatproof dish with melted butter. Sift the flour and 1 tablespoon cocoa into a large bowl and add the sugar. Make a well in the mixture.
2 Beat the egg in a jug and add the milk, melted butter and vanilla essence. Pour the liquid into the dry ingredients and, using a wooden spoon, stir the batter until it is well combined and lump free. Pour into the prepared dish.
3 Combine the brown sugar and the remaining cocoa and sprinkle evenly over the batter. Pour 1 1/2 cups (375 ml/ 12 fl oz) boiling water gently and evenly over the ingredients in the dish. Bake for 30–40 minutes, or until the pudding is cooked—a sauce will have formed underneath. Serve hot with whipped cream or ice cream.

NUTRITION PER SERVE
Protein 6 g; Fat 11 g; Carbohydrate 70 g; Dietary Fibre 1 g; Cholesterol 60 mg; 1640 kJ (390 Cal)

VARIATION: For a crunchy alternative, try adding 1/2 cup (60 g/2 oz) chopped walnuts to the pudding batter before baking.

Add the egg mixture to the dry ingredients and stir with a wooden spoon.

Sprinkle the combined sugar and cocoa over the batter.

Gently pour the boiling water evenly over the pudding.

TRIFLE

Preparation time: 15 minutes + chilling
Total cooking time: 10 minutes
Serves 6

1/2 cup (45 g/1 1/2 oz) flaked almonds
250 g (8 oz) packet jam rollettes (mini jam swiss rolls)
1/3 cup (80 ml/2 3/4 fl oz) dry sherry
2 fresh mangoes or 2 fresh peaches, chopped
2 1/2 cups (600 ml/20 fl oz) ready-made custard
300 ml (9 1/2 fl oz) cream

1 Preheat the oven to moderate 180°C (350°F/Gas 4). Scatter the flaked almonds over a baking tray and cook in the oven for 6–8 minutes, or until golden. Cut the jam rollettes into 1 cm (1/2 inch) slices and place half on the base of a 2.5 litre glass serving bowl.
2 Sprinkle with half the sherry and half the mango or peach. Cover with half the custard. Repeat with the remaining ingredients, then refrigerate until cold.
3 Whisk the cream until stiff peaks form, then spread over the custard and scatter with the toasted almonds.

NUTRITION PER SERVE
Protein 9 g; Fat 27 g; Carbohydrate 45 g; Dietary Fibre 1.5 g; Cholesterol 130 mg; 1920 kJ (460 Cal)

NOTE: If possible, use fresh fruit. If you can't buy fresh, ripe fruit, use a 425 g (14 oz) can of drained peach or mango slices.

Scatter the almonds on a baking tray and cook until golden.

Sprinkle the sherry over the jam rollettes then add the fruit.

Whip the cream until stiff peaks form, then spread it over the custard.

JAM ROLY POLY

Preparation time: 20 minutes
Total cooking time: 35 minutes
Serves 4

2 cups (250 g/8 oz) self-raising flour
125 g (4 oz) butter, roughly chopped
2 tablespoons caster sugar
50 ml (1¾ fl oz) milk
⅔ cup (210 g/7 oz) raspberry jam
1 tablespoon milk, extra

1 Preheat the oven to moderate 180°C (350°F/Gas 4) and line a baking tray with baking paper. Sift the flour into a mixing bowl and, using your fingertips, rub the butter into the flour until the mixture resembles fine breadcrumbs. Stir through the sugar.

2 Add the milk and 50 ml (1¾ fl oz) water, and stir with a flat-bladed knife to form a dough. Turn out onto a lightly floured surface and gather together to form a smooth dough.
3 On a sheet of baking paper, roll out into a rectangle 33 x 23 cm (13 x 9 inches) and 5 mm (¼ inch) thick. Spread with the raspberry jam, leaving a 5 mm (¼ inch) border.
4 Roll up lengthways and place on the tray seam-side down. Brush with the extra milk and bake for 35 minutes, or until golden and cooked. Leave for a few minutes, then slice thickly. Serve warm with custard.

NUTRITION PER SERVE
Protein 7 g; Fat 25 g; Carbohydrate 73 g;
Dietary Fibre 3 g; Cholesterol 80 mg;
2330 kJ (555 Cal)

Rub the butter into the flour with your fingertips until it resembles fine breadcrumbs.

Add the milk and water and mix with a flat-bladed knife to form a dough.

Roll out the dough into a rectangle on a sheet of non-stick baking paper.

Spread the jam over the dough, leaving a border around the edge.

Glossary

Anchovies are a small fish from the herring family found mainly in southern European waters. They are cured and packed in oil, salt or brine and are readily available in cans or jars.

Arborio rice is a special plump, short-grained rice used for making risotto.

Balsamic vinegar is a rich, sweet and fragrant vinegar originating from Modena in Italy. Often used in dressings.

Bicarbonate of soda (baking soda)

Bocconcini are small balls of fresh Italian mozzarella available from delicatessens. Keep refrigerated and covered in the whey in which they are sold for up to 3 weeks. Discard if they show signs of yellowing.

Bok choy (Chinese chard, Chinese white cabbage, pak choi) is a popular Asian green vegetable. The smaller type is called baby bok choy or Shanghai bok choy.

Borlotti beans are slightly kidney-shaped, large, pale pink beans beautifully marked with burgundy specks. They are sometimes available fresh; otherwise canned or dried can be used.

Butternut pumpkin (squash)

Cannellini beans (white beans, Italian white beans) are available canned or dried.

Capsicum (pepper)

Caster sugar (superfine sugar) is a fine white sugar with very small crystals.

Coriander (cilantro, Chinese parsley). All parts of this aromatic plant—seeds, leaves, stem and root—can be eaten.

Cornflour (cornstarch) is a fine white powder that is usually used as a thickening agent.

Eggplants (aubergines) come in a variety of shapes, sizes and colours. Slender eggplants are also called baby, finger or Japanese eggplants, while the most commonly used are larger and rounder.

English spinach (spinach) is sometimes confused with Swiss chard but is much more tender and delicate. It requires little to no cooking but should be washed several times to remove dirt.

Feta cheese is a soft, fresh white cheese ripened in brine. Originally made from the milk of sheep or goats, but often now made with the more economical cow's milk. Feta cheese tastes salty and sharp.

Flat-leaf parsley (Italian parsley, Continental parsley)

Green beans (French beans, string beans)

Icing sugar (confectioners' sugar, powdered sugar). Made by grinding granulated sugar to a fine powder.

Kecap manis is a thick, sweet soy sauce. If unavailable, use regular soy sauce sweetened with a little soft brown sugar.

Lebanese cucumber (short cucumber)

Makrut lime leaves (kaffir lime leaves)

Mince (ground meat)

Olive oil comes in different varieties suitable for different purposes. Extra virgin or virgin olive oil are most commonly used in dressings. Regular olive oils are preferred for cooking because of their neutral flavour. Light olive oil refers to the low content of extra virgin olive oil rather than lightness of calories.

Parmesan cheese is a hard cow's milk cheese used widely in Italian cooking. Sold either grated or in blocks, freshly grated has a much better flavour.

Pecorino cheese is a hard sheep's milk cheese. You can substitute Parmesan cheese.

Plain flour (all-purpose flour)

Prawns (shrimp) are crustaceans which come in various sizes and colours. They become opaque and turn pink once cooked.

Prosciutto is an Italian ham that has been cured by salting then drying in the air. Aged for up to ten months, it is then sliced thinly. It does not require cooking. Prosciutto di Parma is the classic Italian ham traditionally served as an antipasto and also used extensively in cooking.

Roma tomatoes (egg tomatoes, plum tomatoes) are favoured for canning and drying because they have few seeds and a dry flesh. Ideal in sauces and purées. Sometimes called Italian tomatoes.

Self-raising flour (self-rising flour) is plain (all-purpose) flour with baking powder added.

Snow peas (mangetout) are a variety of garden pea, eaten whole after being topped and tailed.

Spring onion (scallion, shallot). These immature onions have a mild, delicate flavour, and both the green tops and the white bulbs can be eaten raw or cooked.

Thick cream (double cream, heavy cream) has a minimum fat content of 48 per cent and some brands have gelatine added to them to give more body.

Tomato paste (tomato purée, double concentrate)

Vanilla essence (vanilla extract) is made by steeping vanilla beans in alcohol and water. Look for products marked natural vanilla or pure vanilla extract and avoid the cheaper synthetic vanilla flavouring, which is made from the chemical artificial vanillan.

Zucchini (courgette)

Index

Published by Murdoch Books®, a division of Murdoch Magazines Pty Ltd.

Murdoch Books® Australia
GPO Box 1203
Sydney NSW 2001
Phone: + 61 (0) 2 4352 7000
Fax: + 61 (0) 2 4352 7026

Murdoch Books UK Limited
Ferry House
51-57 Lacy Road
Putney, London SW15 1PR
Phone: + 44 (0) 20 8355 1480
Fax: + 44 (0) 20 8355 1499

Editorial Director: Diana Hill
Project Manager: Zoë Harpham
Editor: Gordana Trifunovic
Creative Director: Marylouise Brammer
Designer: Michelle Cutler
Production: Fiona Byrne
Recipes developed by the Murdoch Books Test Kitchen.

Chief Executive: Juliet Rogers
Publisher: Kay Scarlett

The Publisher gratefully acknowledges the contribution of the recipe writers, chefs,
photographers and stylists who worked on the material appearing in this publication.

National Library of Australia Cataloguing-in-Publication Data
Everyday family favourites. Includes index. ISBN 1 74045 214 3.
1. Cookery. (Series: Everyday series (Sydney, NSW)).
641.5

IMPORTANT: Those who might be at risk from the effects of salmonella food poisoning
(the elderly, pregnant women, young children and those suffering from immune deficiency diseases)
should consult their GP with any concerns about eating raw eggs.